A BATTLE LOST

Romans and Caledonians
at Mons Graupius

A BATTLE LOST

Romans and Caledonians
at Mons Graupius

GORDON MAXWELL

EDINBURGH UNIVERSITY PRESS

Edinburgh University Press
22 George Square, Edinburgh

Set in Linotronic Times Roman
by Photoprint, Torquay, and
printed in Great Britain by
The Alden Press Limited,
Oxford

British Library Cataloguing
  in Publication Data
Maxwell, Gordon S.
A battle lost: Romans and Caledonians
  at Mons Graupius.
1. Scotland. Army operations by
  Roman Empire armies.
I. Title
936.1'104
ISBN 0 85224 490 8
ISBN 0 85224 615 3 pbk

The publisher acknowledges subsidy from
the Scottish Arts Council towards
the publication of this volume

Contents

Preface

'Ther men mycht se ane hard battale,
And sum defend and sum assale,
And mony a riall rymmyll ryde
Be roucht thair, apon athir syde,
Quhill throu the byrneis brist the blud,
That till the erd doune stremand yhud.'

Barbour, *The Brus*, xii, 555–60

TIMES change. The history that used to be taught in schools, with its
emphasis on lists of kings and dates of battles, has long since given
place to a subject which sets before the student the rich context of
human experience through the ages. Is there still a place, then, for
the study of a single conflict? Or the quest for a lost battlefield? It
might be argued that, since it appears to have neither checked the
course of the Roman occupation of North Britain nor altered the
pattern of local native society, the bloody field of *Mons Graupius*
hardly warrants the attention it has for centuries attracted. But
sentiment, and territorial pride, can dispose of weightier arguments
than these. The Scottish nation has long since taken to its breast the
gallant, if foolhardy, North Britons who made their stand against the
might of Rome in AD 83/4. Not without reason, its antiquaries have
viewed the shadows cast back in time by Bannockburn, Flodden
Field, and Drummossie Muir. For the modern historian, too, the
comparison of Agricola with Edward I, or Cumberland, need not be
without point or profit.

Nor, in modern times, need there be less reason for territorial
pride. The last four decades have seen an accelerating tempo of
discovery by archaeological fieldworkers, excavators, and aerial
surveyors, which has underlined the richness of Scotland's treasury of
Roman monuments. Here, at the limits of Roman conquest, survives
such a variety of military works as is found in few Imperial frontier

provinces. Among them are the camps that may have housed the army destined to fight at *Mons Graupius*, and it is from these that we may one day gain some insight which will allow us to identify the fateful site itself. In the meantime, energy spent upon the quest is not wasted. The more closely we examine the evidence, the better we understand the context of one of the most exciting episodes in British history; moreover, the knowledge gathered here, as often as not, casts light upon problems relating to other sectors of the *Limes*.

We must not forget, however, that these academic studies have their roots in human tragedy on a massive scale. It is important to distinguish between the intellectual problems arising from this tragedy and the human faults which precipitated it. It is not beyond the bounds of probability that the emotions felt by Agricola, as night closed upon the victorious field, were not dissimilar from those experienced by Wellington at Waterloo:

> 'The next greatest misfortune to losing a battle is to gain such a victory as this.'

ACKNOWLEDGEMENTS

The author is grateful to all those colleagues from whom, over the years, he has had the opportunity to learn, by discussion and articles in learned journals, about various aspects of the quest for *Mons Graupius*; for the opinions and interpretations offered here, however, he remains entirely responsible. Acknowledgement should also be made of the encouragement and advice given by Mr Archie Turnbull, former Secretary of the Edinburgh University Press, especially in the presentation of the main text. Both the author and publisher would like to thank the following individuals and institutions for permission to reproduce the undermentioned illustrations: Dr D J Breeze, fig. 11; Cambridge University Committee for Aerial Photography, fig. 29; Hunterian Museum, University of Glasgow, and the Royal Museum of Scotland, Edinburgh, fig. 14; Mr Angus Lamb, fig. 15; Royal Commission on the Ancient and Historical Monuments of Scotland, figs. 2, 7, 8, 27 (Crown Copyright reserved).

Suggested Battlefields

ONE

The Context of the Quest

Our Scottish antiquaries have been greatly divided about the local situation of the final conflict between Agricola and the Caledonians: some contend for Ardoch in Strathallan, some for Innerpeffray, some for the Redykes in the Mearns, and some are for carrying the scene of the action as far north as Blair in Athole.
Scott, *The Antiquary* (1816)

TOWARDS the end of the year AD 97, the Roman historian Tacitus began to write the biography of his wife's father, the peak of whose illustrious career had been a victory over a barbarian army at the world's end. However confidently Tacitus claimed to be writing for posterity, it might have surprised him to learn that more than seventeen centuries after that passage of arms, a writer claiming nominal descent from those same barbarians would amuse half the civilised world by his account of the antiquarian quest for the scene of the conflict. The victor's name was Gnaeus Julius Agricola, the site of the battle was Mons Graupius, and the barbarians were the British tribesmen inhabiting Caledonia. Today, nineteen centuries after the battle, curiosity about the location of the battlefield being undiminished, it may be appropriate to review the changing opinions of generations of scholars on the subject; to consider whether recent advances in archaeological investigation have brought us closer to a solution; and finally, to ask if any other avenues of enquiry are open to us.

The relevance of the issue of Mons Graupius to the study of Roman military activity in Britain will be discussed later, as will the reasons why the topic has continued to engage the attention of historians and archaeologists. But some explanation is required for the prominence accorded to this battle above all others waged in the course of the Roman conquest of North Britain. The answer is simple. Our interest is related directly to the fact that it figures so largely in Tacitus' *Life of Agricola*, which provides the best overall picture of the early Roman occupation of Britain (from AD 43 until 84) available in classical literature.

Tacitus is usually described as an historian, but the *Agricola*, one of the earliest of his works, was written with various ends in view. Its prime purpose was to honour the memory of his father-in-law; but since Agricola had played a leading role in the affairs of his country at home and abroad, there was a deeper, political significance. The latter part of his public life had been acted out against a background of darkening tyranny, and the commemoration of his achievements was possible only because better times had supervened. To be more explicit, the Emperor Domitian was now dead, and the vindictive repressions and persecution that had characterised the second half of his reign were at an end. To his successors, Nerva and Trajan, due compliments might now be paid for restoring long-lost civil liberties and public confidence; and the publication of a work eulogising a man whose virtues had attracted the hatred or fear of Domitian could certainly be so construed. Yet it has been claimed (Dorey 1969, 4–5) that the *Agricola* has another purpose, to explain how the path of duty for those in public life under an unjust ruler did not necessarily lead to outright opposition and ostentatious self-sacrifice: *posse etiam sub malis principibus magnos viros esse*. Tacitus himself, as Domitian's despotism grew to a climax, had progressed through the later stages of a senatorial career, doubtless relying on the *quies* and *obsequium* which he commended in Agricola.

It is unlikely that political considerations influenced the form and content of the work as much as the genre to which it belonged, or rather, the traditions upon which it drew (cf. Ogilvie and Richmond, 1967, 11–20; Dorey 1969, 1–12). The *Agricola* is a curious blend of history and biography, of geography, ethnography, and funeral address, each element accommodating the material of which it is composed to the overall objective of enhancing the glory of the deceased. But only in its character as a belated funeral laudation – Tacitus was abroad when Agricola died in AD 93 – can the value of the work as a source of reliable information be realistically assessed. The style that such an address demanded was rhetorical, and it is not surprising that Tacitus' early training and conspicuous success in public oratory enabled him to construct as elegant a literary memorial as has come down to us from classical antiquity. Even apart from those portions that naturally demanded the declamatory address of the public speaker, the work fairly coruscates with rhetorical artifice (cf. Ogilvie and Richmond 1967, 21–3, 30–1). Yet this is not to say that Tacitus strove to produce little beyond superficial gloss. The variety of treatment and sureness of touch in matters of technical skill should alert us to the possibility that as much painstaking care was lavished on its content as on its form. Behind the brilliant epigrams, beneath the passages of generous prose and occasionally poetic diction, there lay an eminently practical purpose: to persuade the reader of the rightness of Tacitus' versions of events. Of Tacitus' works in general, Miller (1969, 112) has observed that 'style is one of his historical tools', its various elements being used to emphasise the interpretation favoured by the author. In such an approach to history, details and 'facts' may lose the significance we expect them to possess in modern writing. Thus, where the author was striving for effect, there may have been less concern or need for accuracy; the precise number of dead on a battlefield, or the exact strength of an army, may not be required if the situation calls only for the conveying of a general idea – the disparity between the casualties sustained on either side, or the unwonted strength and unanimity of a native alliance in war (cf. Wellesley 1969b). Similarly, the nature of terrain situated at an extreme distance from the Mediterranean world would not have been better appreciated by a Roman audience had Tacitus chosen to reproduce the Celtic names which distinguished the various features of which it was composed. Many have lamented Tacitus' lack of interest in place-names, particularly in Britain (cf. Burn 1969a, 37–40), but it must be admitted that on some occasions, notably in the context of the Agricolan campaigns in Caledonia, their inclusion has left us no wiser.

Although Tacitus could have drawn on memories and records of actual conversations with his father-in-law, not to mention public records available in Rome, the nature of his task, and the style he elected, make it difficult to accept each and every apparently factual statement at face value. On the other hand, the general description of the course of Agricola's campaigns in North Britain and comments on his intentions must owe their form to evidence of an impeccable nature and therefore should be given due consideration. Tacitus may have seemed a garrulous embroiderer (*mendaciorum loquacissimus*) in Tertullian's eyes, but we need not go so far as to believe that he grossly perverted the truth. The historical account he presents in the *Agricola* should therefore be considered to have been based, in his own words, fairly and squarely on the facts (*Agricola*, x, 1: *rerum fide tradentur*), although individual details may have been altered, embellished, or even invented.

The Roman occupation of Britain began in AD 43, roughly a century after the well-known but abortive armed reconnaissance by Julius Caesar. Britain's accessibility from continental Europe as a convenient bolt-hole or asylum for troublemakers within the Empire had long been seen as the most sensible reason for its annexation. Much of the same pretext was later offered by Tacitus for a projected invasion of Ireland ('it would also be of advantage to the Romans in respect of their dealings with Britain, if Roman military strength was on every hand and "liberty" was nowhere to be seen'; *Agricola*, xxxi, 3); similar motives may have lain behind the later attempt to conquer Caledonia. However, other reasons for the initial invasion continued to play a part in deciding imperial policy towards campaigning in Britain. In AD 41 the Emperor Claudius had come to the throne almost by accident, and without any of the prepossessing qualities that might be thought essential in the wielder of supreme power. The invasion of Britain, in which Claudius himself briefly participated, considerably enhanced his reputation, for the island, even after Caesar's campaigns, was considered to be almost fabulously remote and its conquest reckoned an achievement of exceptional skill and daring. A century later, the building of the Antonine Wall and the discomfiture of the northern barbarians may have been intended to add especial lustre to the laurels of another unmilitary emperor, Antoninus Pius (cf. Hanson and Maxwell 1983, 59–64), and long after the Romans had abandoned the island, Procopius could entertain his readers with the picture of an environment north of Hadrian's Wall so hostile that no human being could live there more than half an hour (*de Bellis* viii, 20, 42–55). Although modern dwellers in the home counties might deem the latter account no more than fair comment on the Scottish weather, it is evident that throughout the classical period Britain was considered to possess a magic of its own, and all ventures associated with it were regarded with particular admiration. A like sentiment may have influenced the various emperors who sanctioned the first campaigns in northern Britain, not to mention the soldiers and officers who participated in them. If we are to believe Tacitus' report of the speech with which Agricola encouraged his men at Mons Graupius, the honour of dying for their country was considerably magnified by the remoteness of the field of battle: 'and it will be no disgrace to have perished at the very limit of the natural world' (*Agricola*, xxxiii, 6). Some forty years were to pass, however, before the Roman army extended its dominion from the shores of the English Channel to the approaches to the Moray Firth.

In that interval the Roman province of Britannia had grown at an uneven pace (figure 1): the lowland zone was overrun with relative ease, and by the early 50s the legions were operating in south and central Wales, while a 'pre-emptive strike' by Ostorius Scapula against the Deceangli lying west of the Dee served the double purpose of sundering the Welsh tribesmen from their cousins to the north and east. There were occasional reverses and pauses in this pattern of conquest, and one almost disastrous full-scale revolt in 60/61, when Boudicca, queen of the Iceni, plunged the entire province into bloody chaos before Roman discipline reasserted itself. The recovery of that situation left the army and the principate in no doubt that consolidation of recovered territory was an essential preliminary to any further advance; it proved a lesson that was to reverberate down through the years and be dramatically underlined eight years later on the lower Rhine frontier, when the local Batavian cohorts serving in the army of occupation mutinied. Thereafter, every Roman provincial commander would have been on his guard against unrest in both the civil population and the auxiliary element of his garrison.

Against this background we must see the gradual reduction of resistance in Wales and northern England, the latter theatre of war being the scene of particularly vigorous operations in the later 60s and the first half of the next decade. Two factors combined to concentrate activity in these parts: first was the collapse of the pro-Roman faction at the court of Cartimandua, queen of the Brigantes; second the establishment of the Flavian dynasty on the Imperial

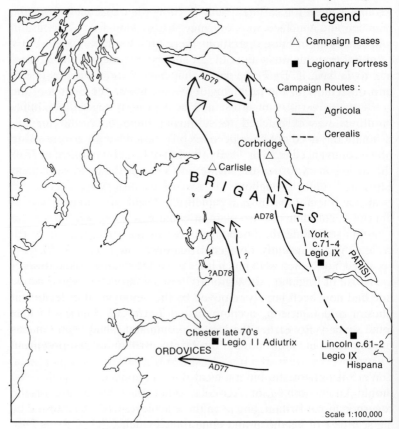

Figure 1. Map showing gradual northward extension of Roman occupation, including early Agricolan campaigns.

throne. After a year of civil strife, in which four emperors had failed to secure their grasp, Vespasian at last established himself in Rome (AD 69), and it may be assumed that he welcomed the opportunity which presented itself in Brigantia of winning a victory that might allow the 'British factor' to add further lustre to his crown. He selected as governor of the province Q. Petillius Cerealis, recent quencher of the Batavian revolt, charging him with the extirpation of all anti-Roman forces in a tribal territory that extended from the Humber and the Dee to the Tyne and Solway. Even Tacitus, in whose account of these operations there breathes an air of hostility, admitted that this was a time of 'great generals, magnificent armies' (*Agricola*, xvii, 1). By 74 the danger had passed and it was possible to turn once more to the problems of Wales, where the Silures of the southern plains were in arms, and no less a strategist than Julius Frontinus was despatched to subjugate them once and for all, although this need not have been his only task during a governorship which commenced in 73 or 74. By the end of his term of office in 77 or 78, the legionary fortresses that were to serve as the main permanent bases in Britain throughout the rest of its history were either in existence or approaching completion. *Legio II Augusta* lay at Caerleon, guarding the rich plain of Glamorgan, *Legio II Adiutrix* at Chester, straddling the boundary between the tribesmen of North Wales and the recently ravaged Brigantes, and *Legio IX Hispana* occupied York, then as in much later times the main garrison town of the North of England. The legionary base at Wroxeter, whose active role had now been largely removed by the deployment of legions at Chester and Caerleon, accommodated *Legio XX Valeria Victrix*; some seven years earlier the legion's commander had been Gnaeus Julius Agricola, who now returned to Britain as its provincial governor.

Were it not for the biographical details supplied by Tacitus, we should know nothing of Agricola, other than his tenure of the governorship of Britain, and even these achievements are attested by the scantiest of historical and epigraphic evidence (cf. Cassius Dio, xxix, 50, 4; xvi, 20, 1–2; *ILS* 8704a). He was born of a well-to-do family in Forumjulii (modern Fréjus in the south of France) on 13 June AD 40. When Agricola was still an infant, his father, Julius Graecinus, was put to death on the orders of the tyrannical Caligula and the boy was brought up by his mother, Julia Procilla. Tacitus tells us that she exercised a moderating influence on him in his youth, particularly during his early education at Marseilles, when the pervading culture of that former Greek colony almost enticed him into a wholly un-Roman pursuit of philosophical studies. Resisting this temptation, he launched out into the ordered routine of ascent through the various grades of Roman public life, known as the *cursus honorum*, in which civil appointments were mingled with military duties. In the course of the latter Agricola became acquainted with Britain even before his appointment to the governorship.

Few governors could have brought with them better qualifications for the job in hand. We know from Tacitus that Agricola had served in Britain as a tribune in 58–61, and had experienced at first hand the critical days of the Boudiccan rising; he had held his legionary command under Petillius Cerealis when all Brigantia resounded to the clash and arms and fierce affrays, not without Roman casualties. Yet there is a tendency among modern scholars (e.g. Dobson 1980; Breeze 1980; Hanson 1987, 39–40) to seek other reasons for this appointment; and it cannot be denied that they exist. Like his two predecessors in the office, Agricola had earned the good favour of Vespasian by his prompt espousal of the Flavian cause in the year of the four emperors. The governorship of Britain can thus be seen as yet another mark of the political support which had brought him the command of *Legio XX*, the governship of Aquitania, and in 77 the consulate at the early age of 37. On the other hand, it may be felt the pendulum of critical reappraisal has now swung a little too far, for there can be little doubt that, when Vespasian made Agricola governor of Britain, he did so with the intention of solving the problem of its northern frontier. Such a solution would have required both the extirpation of intransigent elements among the Brigantes and the removal of any threat posed by hostile tribesmen in the lands beyond, even if it meant campaigning deep within the northernmost regions of the island. It is unlikely that a task of this importance would have been entrusted to an incompetent – or even a mediocre – commander; for Vespasian, who had himself commanded *Legio II Augusta* in Britain during the Claudian invasion, was well aware of the prestigious nature of military operations in that island and knew the propaganda value of reflected glory. Within little more than two years from his assumption of office, Agricola had extended Rome's sphere of influence from the southern fringes of Brigantia to the boundaries of Caledonia, perhaps as far as the shores of the Firth of Tay – a forward leap that must have had the full approval of the emperor and for whose accomplishment Vespasian would surely have expected to take due credit. In fact, since Cassius Dio states (xxxix, 50, 4) that it was Agricola's exploits in Britain which earned Titus,

Vespasian's elder son, his fifteenth salutation as *imperator*, it would seem that the imperial confidence had not been misplaced, even though the fruit of the investment fell to the succeeding emperor.

Any attempt to identify the operations referred to by Cassius Dio leads naturally to the problem of dating Agricola's governorship. Did it commence in AD 77 or 78? The evidence is ambiguous, and there is much to be said on either side (cf. Ogilvie and Richmond 1967, 317–20; Birley 1976; 1981, 73–81; Dobson 1980, 5–11; Hanson 1987, 40–45). All that we can presume with reasonable certainty is that Agricola was appointed *consul suffectus* after a shorter than normal term of office as governor of Aquitania, and arrived back in Rome not later than May 77. After the consulship he gave his daughter in marriage to Tacitus; immediately afterwards he was appointed governor of Britain, entering the province *media aestate*, 'in the middle of the campaigning season', i.e. mid June – mid July, when the garrison was beginning to presume there would be no operations that year (Tacitus, *Agricola* ix, 6; xviii, 1).

Could Agricola have done all that is reported of him and still have arrived in Britain, after a journey of at least three weeks' duration, before the middle of July 77? Everything hinges on the date and nature of the suffect consulship. By the time of Vespasian the consulship was a mere shadow of its former republican glory, when it had represented the highest office of state, held by two citizens for an entire year. It had since become an imperial appointment, with the emperor (and his sons) occupying the post as *consules ordinarii* for the first few months of each year; thereafter a succession of supplementary office-holders (suffect consuls) were selected mainly to top up the reservoir of candidates for administrative or institutional positions requiring consular qualifications. It is thus theoretically possible that Agricola held the abbreviated suffect consulship in 77 immediately or shortly after Vespasian and Titus (or Domitian) – in which case there would have been ample time for him to start on the journey to Britain after his daughter's marriage and still arrive by midsummer in the same year. Indeed, the impression given by Tacitus' account is that Agricola, *despite* having family obligations to discharge after the consulship, nevertheless managed to take up his appointment shortly afterward and *even* continued to lead his troops in the field before the end of that year's campaigning season. Those who argue against the early chronology (e.g. Ogilvie and Richmond 1967, 319–20) stress the strong evidence (Degrassi 1950, 22) against a consulship in 77 before June or July; they point out not only the

Table 1

CORRELATION OF THE EVENTS OF THE GOVERNORSHIP OF JULIUS AGRICOLA W ALTERNATIVE CHRONOLOGIES

	Events in Britain (earlier chronology)	Imperial Affairs	Events in Britain (later chronology)	
AD77	Agricola to Britain *media aestate*: 1st campaign against Ordovices.	Agricola *consul suffectus* (possibly AD76): Tacitus weds Agricola's daughter.		AD'
AD78	2nd campaign *Aestuaria ac silvas*		Agricola to Britain *media aestate*: 1st campaign against Ordovices.	AD'
AD79	3rd campaign, *novas gentes . . . usque ad Taum*	23 June Vespasian dies; Titus succeeds	2nd campaign *Aestuaria ac silvas*	AD'
AD80	4th campaign *inventus terminus . . . Clota et Bodotria*		3rd campaign *Novas gentes . . . usque ad Taum*	AD&
AD81	5th campaign *nave prima . . . Hiberniam*	13 September Titus dies; Domitian succeeds	4th campaign *inventus terminus . . .Clota et Bodotria*	AD&
AD82	6th campaign *amplexus civitates trans Bodotriam*		5th campaign *nave prima . . . Hiberniam . . .*	AD&
AD83	7th campaign *Mons Graupius . . . exacta iam aestate*	Domitian campaigns against Chatti: ? Chattan triumph (autumn) ?	6th campaign *amplexus civitates trans Bodotriam*	AD&
AD84	? Agricola leaves Britain Jan./Feb.?		7th campaign *Mons Graupius . . . exacta iam aestate*	AD&

Table 1
(CONTINUED)

Events in Britain (earlier chronology)	Imperial Affairs	Events in Britain (later chronology)	
	? early in year? Oppius Sabinus defeated and killed in Moesia in Dacian invasion	? Agricola leaves Britain Jan./Feb.?	AD85
? Legionary fortress at Inchtuthil abandoned? ? Legio II Adiutrix withdrawn from province	Roman punitive expedition crosses Danube and is disastrously defeated	? Legionary fortress at Inchtuthil abandoned? ? Legio II Adiutrix withdrawn from province	AD86
? Legionary fortress at Inchtuthil abandoned?		? Legionary fortress at Inchtuthil abandoned?	AD87

improbability of so crowded a timetable being completed within the first half of the year, but also the difficulties that arise in harmonising a correspondingly early end to Agricola's term of office with events elsewhere in the Empire (see Table 1 and pp. 114–16 below). There is, moreover, the problem of explaining what happened in the correspondingly longer interval between Agricola's departure from Britain and the wholesale abandonment of the outermost frontier installations, which can be dated by archaeological evidence to AD 86 or 87. On the other hand, it is also possible that Agricola's consulship fell in the latter part of AD 76 (Campbell 1986) and the urgency detectible in Tacitus' account related to the hustle and bustle of the marriage arrangements.

For the present purpose it will be enough to identify the several campaigns of Agricola by reference to the year of his governorship, the question of date being raised only where it is relevant to a discussion of the operation in hand; a review of the chronology is provided in the last chapter, where the relationship of the Flavian conquest to the wider history of Roman Scotland is examined in more detail.

Tacitus tells us that Agricola conducted seven annual campaigns during his long term of office, of which only the two last appear to have been directed specifically against the tribes of Caledonia, who evidently provided him with his fiercest opposition. The first campaign, mounted comparatively late in the season, took the form of a punitive expedition against the Ordovices of North Wales, who had just wiped out a cavalry regiment stationed in their territory (*Agricola*, xviii). If we are to believe Tacitus, Agricola's retaliatory measures bordered upon genocide (*caesaque prope universa gente*), but there is no archaeological evidence for such drastic action, and recourse has perhaps been made to literary hyperbole – a point to bear in mind when considering the account of casualties at Mons Graupius. In the second year, there was evidently much activity: marauding and rallying, building bivouacs, reconnaissance of a land characterised by estuaries and forests, alternating use of the iron fist and the velvet glove to such good effect that 'many tribes previously independent, abandoned their hostile attitude', and, with hostages and warrants for their good behaviour, allowed themselves to be wound within the shroud of the Roman frontier-system (*Agricola*, xx). There is no specific indication in the text of the identity of these tribes or the location of the 'estuaries and forests', but it seems probable that the north of England was the theatre of operations and that the northernmost septs of the Brigantes were those now brought formally within the province (cf. Potter 1979, 356–8). The easiest solution may be to interpret the vague terms of the Tacitean description as little more than a literary 'topos', or decorative episode, serving as a smokescreen to conceal a season of relatively little forward progress but much consolidation of the conquests of predecessors.

If the operations in which Agricola had himself participated as legionary legate under Cerealis had extended north of the Solway and the Cheviots, this might help to explain the rapidity of movement in the next stage of Agricola's advance. Certainly, reference to new tribes encountered in that year, the third of his governorship, would seem to support such a view, and the information that the land was wasted as far north as the estuary of a river known as the *Tavus* or *Tava* – which is usually identified as the Tay (cf. Rivet and Smith 1979, 470), but which may possibly have been the Teith, or some more southerly river estuary (Maxwell 1984b, 1988) – confirms that Agricola now penetrated or approached the southern borders of Caledonia. It is clear from Tacitus (*Agricola* xxii) that he did so with relative ease, the British tribes in these parts offering very little resistance despite the fact that the elements were on their side, assailing the Roman columns with the pluvial armoury of an average Scottish summer (*saevis tempestatibus*); as a result, before the season closed, there was even time for the construction of certain permanent forts, which, it is implied, would not normally have been built until the following year.

Not surprisingly, the fourth season was used to consolidate the Roman hold on the territory over which they had so expeditiously advanced. The building of further permanent forts, *castella*, would now have been put in hand, but the description of events given by Tacitus (*Agricola*, xxiii) makes it clear that the governor's main concern was with establishing a secure frontier against the northern tribes. Fortunately, an ideal geographical position offered itself in the Forth-Clyde isthmus, whose suitability for the purpose Agricola would already have learned from reconnaissance. Posting a chain of garrisons on this narrow neck of land, Agricola then turned to the occupation of the hinterland. There was much to be done even if only the south of Scotland were to be brought to a state of dependable quiescence.

Many scholars have interpreted the enigmatic description of the fifth year's campaigning (*Agricola* xxiv) as an account of further tidying-up operations in the South-West. The crucial phrase in Tacitus' description occurs in the opening sentences: 'Agricola crossed over in the first ship (*nave prima transgressus*) and, in a string of successful battles, subdued tribes who had never been heard of till then; and he stationed troops in that part of Britain which faces Ireland . . .'. Once more the historian's lack of interest in proper names deprives us of the identity of the conquered peoples, but even allowing for that, there is an abruptness which suggests that the text of the *Agricola*, as it has come down to us, is deficient. In particular, it has been suggested that the name of a river or estuary should be supplied after *transgressus*; the proposals are many and various. For those who believe that the context justifies the presumption of a naval operation originating in the Forth-Clyde isthmus, the Firth of Clyde seems most attractive, but there is a difference of opinion regarding the objective – possibly the Ayrshire coast (Ogilvie and Richmond 1967, 235), or even the coastal districts of Argyll (Reed 1971). It is improbable that the scene of the battles was distinct from the shores on which the projected Irish invasion-force was assembled and the latter can hardly be other than those at Ayrshire or Galloway. Yet, if the south-west of Scotland was the theatre of operations in the fifth campaign, and there is every reason to believe that this was an area into which it would have been logical, and indeed necessary, to move after the sweeping advance to the *Taum aestuarium* and the establishment of the Forth-Clyde frontier, we may well agree with Wellesley (1969a) that 'no Roman commander in his senses would invade south-west Scotland by sea when he could move on dry land'. Consequently, suggestions that the missing word is *Itunam* (the Solway) command little more acceptance, and even Richmond's *Anavam* (the Annan) or *Novium* (the Nith), neither of which involves gross emendation of the text, can still be objected to as hardly justifying a major naval operation. Indeed, in view of the claims that Tacitus makes for Agricola's use of naval forces in the following season (see below, p. 23), it may be argued that the passage is not only deficient but also corrupt, with no original reference to the use of ships, unless it was in connection with the possible invasion of Ireland. Recent discoveries about the character of large marching-camps at Dalswinton in Nithsdale and Castledykes in Clydesdale (Maxwell and Wilson 1987, 30–32) make it probable that in this year the main thrust was directed westwards from those bases. It has been suggested (Maxwell 1989a, 54) that *nave prima* is a corrupt form of *in avia primum*, a reference to the trackless wastes that would have to be crossed between the start-line and the rich coastal districts of the Clyde.

The Irish campaign, however, was not to be. When the season opened in the following year, the legions had orders to march north across the Forth, and the two-year-long campaign against the Caledonians was under way. Tacitus gives no reason for this sudden change of direction, but it represents a policy decision that must have been taken at the highest level, for, as we shall see, it committed the Roman army to a programme of conquest and occupation in that part of Britain that successive episodes of history have shown to be hazardous ground for invading armies from the south (cf. Maxwell 1984a). Whoever took the decision must have realised its implications and been willing to pay the eventual cost, in other words, the emperor himself. It is tempting, therefore, to see this vigorous change of policy as evidence of a new hand on the tiller, a situation that accords better with the early chronology of Agricola's governorship (Table 1). It would not be unreasonable to suggest therefore that Domitian, who became emperor on 13 September 81, had a very real personal interest in the successful prosecution of the Caledonian campaign, as it would have been among the first full-scale operations to which he gave his blessing. It is also important to realise that this implies an interest that continued beyond the governorship of Agricola.

So much for the evidence provided by Tacitus in his account of the years preceding *Mons Graupius*. The testimony of archaeology is less explicit, especially in the matter of dating, the choice no longer being between one year and another but almost between different decades. It is important that this point be appreciated, for the identification of 'Agricolan' forts and marching-camps in North Britain often depends more on a presumed relationship to the campaigns of Agricola as reported by Tacitus than on the limited data available from excavation. The nature of this problem has been reviewed by several scholars in recent times (cf. for general historical purposes. Hanson 1980a, 1987, 135–6; for the Agricolan date of permanent forts, Breeze 1980, Frere 1980a; for temporary camps, Hanson 1980b, Maxwell 1980, 1982).

Evidence for the campaigning – the movement of troops described by Tacitus – is presumed to be supplied by temporary structures known as marching-camps, most of which are now identifiable only through the medium of air reconnaissance (figure 2). Temporary camps were used by the Roman army for many purposes and at all periods of the occupation of North Britain, and the assigning of any particular site to the Agricolan period is hedged around with difficulties. Strictly speaking, only those camps that have produced unequivocal evidence of early date should be considered, and, until recently, in Scotland south of the Forth only two camps, one of roughly 19 hectares, another of 16 hectares, at Newstead qualified for

Figure 2. Air photograph of the Agricolan marching camp at Stracathro revealed by cropmarks; note the elaborate gateway defence and outside the camp, a native ring-ditch house with possible souterrain.

this description; further to the south in Redesdale the 18-hectare camp at Silloans, which was clearly in existence before the building of the great north-south arterial route, Dere Street, could also be assigned to an early period. Many temporary camps have been discovered beside this road, which provided the most direct access from northern England to the shores of the Forth, and the identification of what appears to be a Flavian supply depot at Red House, near Corbridge, the southern terminal of that route (Hanson, Daniels, *et al.* 1979), makes it probable that this was one of Agricola's main corridors of invasion in the third season.

Elsewhere, we are dependent on a distinctive structural element by which to recognise camps that may have held the Flavian army – the gateway defence known as the *clavicula*. This device took the form of a quarter-circle of ditch or rampart extending the defences of the

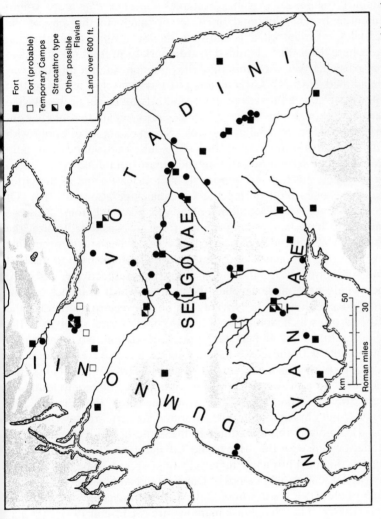

Figure 3. Map of South and Central Scotland showing probable Agricolan forts and temporary camps with native tribal areas.

camp across the inside or outside of the entrance (or occasionally both), in such a way as to force an attacking enemy to expose his right-hand side (unprotected by the shield) to the defenders on the rampart (figure 2); in some examples the *claviculae* were complemented by an additional ditch set obliquely to the axis of the defences, a variant which is known as the 'Stracathro' type, after the site where it was first identified in cropmark form from the air. As at that particular site the camp underlies the annexe of a fort that was abandoned *c*.AD 86–7, there are good reasons for believing that gateways of this kind very probably indicate an origin in the Flavian period, although this does not necessarily mean that their construction was put in hand by Agricola. Seven examples of camps with *claviculae* have so far been recorded in southern Scotland, and there are several more in northern England, apart from those recorded on Dere Street, but it is not impossible that at least some of the latter may have been built during the Cerealian operations of 71–4. Of those located in the southern uplands of Scotland, four are large enough to have held a campaigning force of considerable size, the largest, Dalswinton and Castledykes (*c*.24 hectares), occupying positions of great tactical and strategic importance astride routes that lead westwards into Galloway and Ayrshire respectively. As such, they would have made excellent bases from which to launch a twin-pronged assault upon the Novantae of South-western Scotland in the fifth season, which would imply that Agricola's total strength in the field required some 48 hectares of accommodation. No other camps comparable with these two have so far been discovered in southern Scotland, but it has been pointed out (RCAHMS 1978, 34) that the combined area of two categories of camp, one commonly found on Dere Street and the Annandale-Clydesdale route, the other used by Roman units moving along the intermediate cross-routes (figures 3 and 4), amounts to approximately the same figure. When we seek similar evidence for the drive to the Tay in the latter part of the third season, the most attractive material would appear to be provided by the two large marching-camps of Dunning and Abernethy on the south bank of the River Earn, whose Flavian date is indicated by the associated pottery of South Gaulish manufacture (St Joseph 1973, 218–21).

The area occupied by each of the last-named camps – 47 and 46 hectares respectively – approximates so closely to the combined area

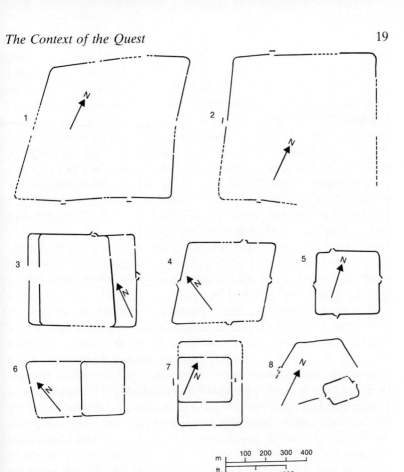

Figure 4. Plans of probable Agricolan temporary camps: 1, Abernethy;
2, Dunning; 3, Castledykes; 4, Stracathro; 5, Dalginross; 6, Ardoch;
7, Dunblane; 8, Woodhead.

of camps presumed to have been used simultaneously in other stages
of the invasion that it is difficult not to believe that these extremely
large works contained almost the entire force that Agricola was able
to dispose in the field during the early years of his governorship.
Unfortunately, there is no way of calculating precisely how many
troops such bivouacs might have held. Estimates of the capacity of

temporary camps vary from around 600 men per hectare to about 1200 (Grillone 1977, xi–xvi; Hanson 1978), but the actual figure probably depended on the ratio of legionary troops to auxiliaries, the proportion of cavalry among the auxiliary forces, and the length of occupation contemplated by the camp builders. Conservative estimates would therefore put the strength of Agricola's field army at about 42,500 men divided equally between auxiliary units and the legions, with cavalry composing roughly half the *auxilia*; this, or perhaps a slightly higher figure, say 50,000, would not be unreasonable for a provincial garrison that has been thought to number at most ninety auxiliary regiments (Frere 1978, 135–6), particularly if we consider that a certain proportion of the force would have been required to maintain security in recently pacified rearward areas, like Wales and the north of England; by the second half of Agricola's governorship even this figure would have been trimmed by the need to send detachments overseas (see below, pp. 30–1).

By the end of the fifth campaign, moreover, a number of permanent forts had been established in southern Scotland, whose safekeeping required at least caretaker garrisons. Foremost among these will have been the stations on the Forth-Clyde isthmus, which archaeology is just beginning to identify. It was previously thought that the remains of this frontier chain would be found beneath forts of the Antonine Wall (Macdonald 1934, 396) but the discovery from the air of a small Flavian fort at Mollins (figure 5), some way to the south of the line occupied by the second-century *limes* (Hanson and Maxwell 1980), revealed that the two lines need not have been wholly coincident. Although the situation still awaits clarification, it seems probable that at least part of Agricola's frontier consisted of a series of *castella* in which perhaps small posts and normal cohort-forts alternated at intervals of about six Roman miles. Artefactual evidence of Flavian date recovered from the Wall forts at Cadder and Castlecary on either side of Mollins, as well as at Mumrills further to the east, indicate where this early frontier, one of the first to be mentioned in the history of Imperial defensive-systems, afforded protection to the fledgling province to the south. How far it extended across the isthmus cannot yet be ascertained, but it has been suggested (Hanson 1980b) that its western terminus may have lain on the right bank of the Clyde near its confluence with the River Kelvin, and on the east it could have stretched along a succession of inland ridges as far as the Lothian Esk; its right and left flanks could then have rested on the territories of the apparently less hostile southern tribes, the Votadini and the Dumnonii. The recent discovery of a Flavian bridgehead fort at Doune on the River Teith (Maxwell 1984b), at the eastern end of a chain extending possibly as far as Dumbarton on the Clyde estuary, may indicate, however, that a second defensive system was drawn across the waist of Scotland at this time. How it related to the presumed southern chain, complementing or replacing it, cannot be determined (cf. Jarrett 1985, 61–2).

It would be reasonable to assume, however, that the majority of the fort-sites indicated on figure 3 were either occupied, or at some stage of construction, by the time the order came for the renewal of the northward advance. In recent years, aerial survey has identified a temporary work that may cast a ray of light on this less glamorous aspect of frontier warfare, for it has been suggested that the camp of Woodhead, on Dere Street south of Dalkeith (figure 4), may have been the base of a logging detachment amassing the raw material needed to build Agricola's new forts (Maxwell 1983b). On the plateau beside the camp, which was only 1.5 ha in area, there was a large polygonal enclosure where the cut timber may have been stacked, the entrances of both works being protected by *claviculae* of the Stracathro type, a strong indication that they were used in the early Flavian period, quite possibly in the unexpected calm that followed Agricola's first drive to the *Tava aestuarium*. When next he came, as will be seen in chapter two, the mood of the inhabitants of Caledonia had turned from stupefied inactivity to aggressive resistance. The people of the north were now determined to fight for their freedom.

TWO

On the Threshold of Caledonia

WITH the whole of southern Scotland securely held, either by force of conquest or the sheer weight of garrisons in occupation, Agricola could begin to make his plans for extending the power of Rome over the country that lay to the north of the Forth-Clyde isthmus. Some reconnaissance had already been carried out. Plutarch mentions (*de defectu oraculorum*, 18, 419e–420a; Burn 1969b, 2–4) a schoolmaster, Demetrius of Tarsus, who had taken part in an imperially-sponsored reconnaissance among the islands off the coast of Britain at some time shortly before AD 83. From the brief description of these islands it would seem probable that they included the Western Isles; hence it is not unreasonable to assume that the expedition may have been associated with Agricola's fifth campaign, when naval operations against Ireland were contemplated. One of the fruits of this reconnaissance, which is clearly reflected in Tacitus' description of the heavily indented west coast of Scotland, with its winding sea-lochs in the very heart of the Highland hills, was that Roman military intelligence at least knew that northward advance by land along the western side of the country was out of the question.

Of the character and extent of the terrain that lay before him on the east, however, it is likely that Agricola knew comparatively little. Just a hint of the daunting uncertainty of the prospect filters through the terse prose of Tacitus; for example, in his description of the country north of the narrow central isthmus, to which the name Caledonia is applied (*Agricola*, x, 3): 'but when you cross over into Caledonia, there is a vast shapeless tract of country stretching on and on beyond the shore (at the estuary) that itself had seemed to be the furthest limit of the island'; or in the words put into the mouth of the Caledonian commander at *Mons Graupius* (xxxii, 2), scorning the apparently hapless Roman army who 'gazed around panic-stricken at the strangeness of it all, the sea, the woods, the very sky itself like nothing that they knew'. In fact, it would seem that this quality of the unknown was an ingredient in the success of Agricola's forces, their discipline and martial spirit responding to the challenge of a conflict against the odds, when even to lose would produce a sort of glory. It is probable that, despite the existence of so many imponderable factors, Agricola had already set himself a target, a limit of penetration or conquest, which intelligence gathered during the two previous seasons might have shown to be readily attainable. Before discussing the degree to which that objective may have been attained, it would be best to consider the evidence, in particular the full written account.

Agricola, 25: Now in the campaigning season that marked the beginning of his sixth year of office, Agricola overran the territory of those tribes that lived beyond the Forth, and because it was feared that there might be a general rising among the peoples living beyond them and that communications might be threatened by enemy action, he sent out the fleet to reconnoitre suitable landing-places. The fleet was now used for the first time as part of an operational force, and in its supporting role made a grand spectacle, since the war was being prosecuted on both land and sea simultaneously. Often units of infantry, cavalry and shipborne troops mingled in the same bivouacs, sharing their rations and their high spirits, as each made much of their respective deeds and adventures; in turn they boasted, as soldiers will, comparing the hidden depths of tree-clad mountain ranges with the hazards of storms at sea; there were tales on the one hand of beaten foes and captured territory, on the other of the conquest of Ocean. As for the British tribesmen, it was learned from prisoners of war that the sight of the fleet left them thunderstruck, because it seemed that by opening the recesses of a sea they looked on as their defence, we had cut off their last means of escape in defeat.

The tribes of Caledonia got ready to fight with great preparation of equipment, all of which was exaggerated by rumour, as usually happens when real information is in short supply. They even launched attacks on some forts and, by taking the offensive, increased the feeling of panic. The faint-hearted on the Roman side, under the guise of caution, were actually advising Agricola to retire south of the Forth before the army was driven back in defeat, when news came to him that an enemy force comprising several independent columns was about to attack. But Agricola, fearing that the enemy might use their superior numbers and better knowledge of the territory to outflank him, divided his army into three groups and, taking personal command, advanced to meet them.

Agricola, 26: When the enemy got to know this, they suddenly changed their plans and joined forces for a night attack on the Ninth Legion, since it was the weakest of the three. They slew the camp sentries and burst in, amidst scenes of panic and sleep-befuddled confusion; in fact, there was a battle raging actually inside the camp, when Agricola, who had learned from patrols about the enemy movement and had followed hard on their tracks, gave the order for the swiftest of the cavalry and infantry to fall upon the Caledonian rear; presently he told the whole of the force to start shouting, and as they did so their standards caught fire in the light of approaching day. Thus the Britons were terrified by the threat of an attack on two fronts, and the men of the Ninth Legion, recovering their spirit, cast aside fears for their safety and began to compete for a share of the honours. They even broke out of the position into which they had been penned, and there was some fierce fighting in the very passage of the entrance to the camp until the enemy were driven off, each of the legions vying with the other, one side to play the part of the successful rescuer, the other to seem to have been in no need of any help whatsoever! Both were doubtless of the opinion that if only the fleeing Britons had not escaped into the surrounding morasses and forests, that victory could have brought the war to an end.

Agricola, 27: Their spirits ablaze with the realisation of what they had done, or what they had heard about the action, Agricola's troops now felt that no task was too great for their courage. They clamoured that they should push on into the heart

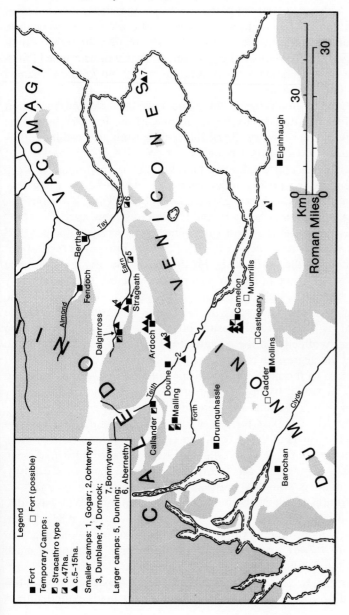

Figure 5. Map of Scotland between Forth and Tay showing presumed early (Agricolan) forts and temporary camps.

of Caledonia and fight their way to the uttermost limits of Britain. Of course, those who just a little while ago had been so cautious and prudent, after the victory, made a big show of their eagerness. And this is the most unjust aspect of war: when things are going well, everybody takes the credit, but failure is blamed on one man alone.

On the other hand, the British tribes reckoned that their defeat was due not to the superiority of the Romans but to the luck of the draw and Agricola's generalship. Accordingly, they had lost none of their haughty self-confidence, but, packing off their wives and children to places of safety, continued to keep their young warriors under arms and solemnised the tribal war-league with sacrifices and ritual assemblies. Thus, with spirits at fever-pitch on either side, the combatants drew apart.

This description of the sixth campaign begins with an uncharacteristically explicit reference to the field of operations: the territory of tribes living to the north of the Forth. Unfortunately, it is not made clear how far to the north, nor is it certain whether the introductory phrase summarises all the action of this year or refers only to the preliminary stage. The use of the fleet in an operational role – made much of by Tacitus (and presumably Agricola) – would have been particularly effective if the estuaries of Forth and Tay had been the scene of the aggressive reconnaissance described in chapter 25. Even if the drive to the north in the third campaign had actually reached the Tay, it would hardly have afforded opportunity for adequately exploring either the hills and glens of what is now Central Region, or the relatively complex terrain of the Fife peninsula. No advance beyond the Tay could have been contemplated without both of these areas being thoroughly investigated; indeed, until Fife had been effectively neutralised, the security of the right flank of the Forth-Clyde chain of *praesidia* must have remained in the balance – a consideration to which the builders of the Antonine Wall gave due attention some sixty years later (Hanson and Maxwell, 1983, 101–3). These arguments apply even more strongly if, as has been suggested (Maxwell 1984b), Agricola had not previously advanced much beyond the Teith.

If we are to believe Ptolemy, the western portion of Central Scotland was occupied by the Dumnonii, whose lands extended from

Kyle and Carrick and Upper Clydesdale northwards, perhaps as far as Strathearn (figure 5); the settlements or forts situated in their midst include *Vindogara* (probably Irvine) and *Alauna* (probably Ardoch) (Ptolemy II, 3, 7). Fife probably belonged in the main to *Venicones* (*pace* Rivet and Smith 1979, 490–1) whom Ptolemy described (II, 3, 9) as situated 'below and to the west of' – in fact to the south and east of – tribes probably living in Aberdeenshire and Strathmore. Although these tribesmen were doubtless included in the peoples whom Tacitus had described as the 'hostile elements banished as it were to another island' by the chain of *praesidia* on the isthmus (*Agricola*, xxiii), the real trouble now originated in 'the tribes living beyond', which we may take to indicate the population of the regions to the north of the Earn and the Tay, whom Ptolemy knew as the *Vacomagi* and *Taexali* (figures 5 and 9), but Tacitus calls simply 'the inhabitants of Caledonia'.

The location of Caledonia and the tribal group known variously as *Caledones* or *Caledonii* has been the matter of debate. For some time now, it has been presumed (cf. Maxwell 1975, 41–6), and more recently argued in detail (Hind 1983), that the name was applied generally by classical writers to most of the land-mass and tribal groupings to the north of the Forth-Clyde isthmus. Hence we read of a Caledonian *silva* or *saltus* for the wild, mountain fastnesses, a Caledonian *angulus*, for the northern capes, and possibly a *Caledonian Ocean* laving its western shore (if Ptolemy's *Duecaledonius* (II, 3, 1) is a misreading of an original Latin text mentioning *Oceanus Hyperboreus sive Caledonius*). It is interesting that although a separate tribe named the *Caledonii* is mentioned in Ptolemy (II, 3, 8), and located by him in what approximates to either the Great Glen or the Grampian massif, Tacitus always uses the periphrastic form *Caledoniam incolentes*, as here, or *Caledoniam habitantium* (xi, 2), or else refers to them as *Britanni*. Over a century later, the two main enemies of Rome in North Britain are identified as the Caledonians and the *Maeatae* (Cassius Dio, lxxvi, 12), the latter living next to the 'cross-wall that cuts the island in two' with the Caledonians beyond, i.e. to the north of them. By this time the names represented confederacies that had swallowed up lesser clans, and by the end of the third century the Caledonians in turn had been absorbed into the Pictish peoples, although even in the later fourth century, under the name *Dicalydones*, they appear to have formed one of the two main divisions of the *Picti* (Ammianus Marcellinus, xxviii, 8, 4). Since the other division, the *Verturiones*, may have given their name to the historical region of Fortrenn, which encompassed Strathearn and Menteith, it may be presumed that the *Dicalydones* were their northern neighbours.

The evidence of proto-history and linguistics, although relatively insubstantial, thus combines to suggest that during much of the first millennium AD the native peoples living in eastern Scotland north of the Forth belonged to confederacies, no doubt often loosely-knit, of which the most important was that known either as the Caledonians (or some related form), or else 'the peoples of Caledonia'. Moreover, although the name Caledonia might be loosely applied to the whole land mass north of the Forth-Clyde isthmus, the southern boundary of the Caledonian heartland probably lay nearer the Tay than the Forth. In recent years various attempts have been made to put archaeological flesh on these bones, but the major drawback is the relative paucity of explicit evidence, particularly in terms of settlement archaeology. Most writers have stressed the manifest cultural differences that may be recognised to the south of the Forth and the north of the Tay, but lack of material has made the drawing of precise cultural boundaries a task fraught with difficulties. Nevertheless, the apparent permanence of certain patterns of distribution merits close consideration. Particular interest attaches to the southern boundary of distribution of artefacts and monuments as widely dispersed in time and character as carved stone balls of secondary Neolithic origin (Marshall 1977), bronze ornate bracelets of the second or third century AD (MacGregor 1976, 103–17), and Pictish Symbol Stones of Classes I and II (Wainwright 1956, 97–101); or square barrow cemeteries (Maxwell 1983c; 1987, 34–5), souterrains (Wainwright 1963; Maxwell 1987, 36–42), unenclosed settlements of round timber houses (Maxwell 1983d, 246–8), and place-names incorporating the element *pit-* (Whittington 1975). The consistency with which these patterns of distribution are bounded on the south by a line that runs south-eastwards from the middle reaches of the Tay near Dunkeld to the north shore of the Firth of Forth in the neighbourhood of Kirkcaldy – with a possible salient extending a little way into Strathearn – illustrates dramatically the problems facing Agricola in his penultimate campaign. For in graphic form it demonstrates the tug-of-war to which the middle ground between Forth and Tay has been subjected at all periods of pre- and proto-history, at some times falling under the influence of the Caledonian north, at others dominated by possibly wealthier nations to the south. Although this ambiguous position has been suspected for some time (cf. Maxwell 1969, 105–8; 1975, 41–7), recent more intensive study of settlement sites in selected areas of eastern Scotland (Macinnes 1982) has suggested that during the later first century AD the Fife peninsula had temporarily established closer ties with its southern neighbours.

The present state of the evidence does not permit us to expound upon the nature of those ties. It is therefore likely that Tacitus' claims that 'the red hair and massive limbs of the inhabitants of Caledonia indicate an origin in Germany' (*Agricola*, xi, 2) are based upon accurate observation by Agricola, or his comrades in arms, of real ethnic differences in the native population; and this is further borne out by the basically non-Celtic forms of those names attributed by Ptolemy to the tribes of Scotland between the Forth and the Moray Firth and to the settlements situated in their midst (Jackson 1956, 136), a fact that, along with the evidence of modern place-names, has led most scholars to accept that the inhabitants of Caledonia would have spoken a language related to, but appreciably different from, that used by the Brythonic-speaking peoples to the south.

There are reasonably good grounds for believing that, in the preliminary stages of his northward advance from the Forth-Clyde isthmus, Agricola could have been concerned to secure the area lying on his left flank against possible infiltration from the highlands to the west and north. It would have been prudent to establish at least semi-permanent garrison-posts at tactically or strategically important points, possibly with the additional purpose of protecting tribesmen of the Dumnonii, kinsmen or heirs of those who occupied the palisaded homesteads recently identified in this area (Maxwell 1983a). It has already been suggested (p. 20) these posts may have been constructed at the end of the fourth campaign, extending occupied territory to the foothills of Caledonia. The case of Ardoch, where the strongly defended Flavian and Antonine fort site is adjoined by an enclosure of more than temporary build and about 1.5 ha in area, should alert us to the probability that more of these presumably early and lightly-defended structures await discovery. Agricola's troops may have been engaged in their construction as the fleet began its task of coastal reconnaissance; it can easily be imagined how alarming this naval presence in the Firths of Forth and Tay would have been to the natives of Fife, whose allegiance lay with their Caledonian confederates to the north, as they saw the Roman forces also consolidating their hold on lands lying immediately to the west. (The small coastal camps at Dun, on the Montrose Basin, and at East Haven, south of Arbroath, need not belong to this phase of operations, for which larger installations might be thought appropriate. In the course of active campaigning, however, desperate measures could have dictated otherwise.)

It was at this juncture that news came of the enemy's approach in strength – the verb *inrupturos* implying an invasion launched from Caledonia proper into the region north of the Forth-Clyde *praesidia* where Agricola's men were already operating. It may seem curious that Agricola's reply to this assault was to divide his forces, since we have reason to believe that these were already weakened by having to provide *vexillations* to serve on the Continent (see below, p. 31). But his motives in doing so were doubtless twofold: firstly, by interposing a screen of units, to prevent the Caledonian columns getting across the Forth into territory where there was probably no mobile reserve, and to commit the enemy forces to a pitched battle, in which, even against superior numbers, a Roman army was almost bound to be victorious.

The identification of archaeological traces of the subsequent conflict and the steps that led up to it is not an entirely insoluble problem, although, once more, for lack of material evidence, little progress can yet be reported. Nevertheless, if we are right in estimating that all Agricola's field-forces of the previous campaigns could be accommodated inside a marching-camp of about 47 hectares, it would be reasonable to assume that a tripartite division would have resulted in three series of camps, none of which exceeded 16 hectares. For various reasons, it seems likely that all the camps were in fact appreciably smaller. The depleted state of Agricola's army is implied in Tacitus' use of the phrase *maxime invalida* to describe the battle-group of the Ninth Legion; all were under strength, but the Ninth, where the others may have contributed only a single cohort for service on the continent, could have been deprived of as many as 1,500 men (cf. Dobson 1980, 9) detached for service under the tribune Roscius Aelianus during the *expeditio Germanica* (Birley 1981, 270). An alternative explanation of the exceptional weakness of the Ninth made long ago by Syme (1932, 111, n. 17) is that the location of that legion's fortress at York, on the fringes of the newly-conquered north of England, made it necessary for a higher proportion of its strength to be retained for garrison duties at base. In view of the long history of stubborn resistance by the tribes of Wales, however, it may fairly be asked if the other legions, stationed in Chester, Wroxeter and Caerleon did not labour under the same obligations.

The result of these contingencies was that Agricola's army corps had been reduced by around 3,000 legionaries (and possibly a comparable number of auxiliaries), conceivably a fifth of the resources previously available to him on campaign. The fact that Tacitus gives the epithet *nonani* (men of the Ninth) to the weakest of the contingents into which Agricola divided his army does not *necessarily* mean that only three of the four legions based in Britain were engaged in the Caledonian campaign; two of the others could have 'doubled up' in the same group. Yet it seems unlikely that this would have occurred, unless the two units in question had been appreciably weaker than the Ninth, and this, in view of the obligations incurred by the latter legion, is scarcely credible. In short, the only good reason for dividing a force into three unequal elements is that they were all originally independent units, designed to fight and function on their own. If, therefore, only three of the four legions were available, it may be that the reduction in Agricola's battle group compared with previous years was proportionally greater than suggested above.

In its entirety this weakened army could have been accommodated in a marching-camp of about 35 hectares; when divided into three separate divisions the resulting bivouacs would naturally have been much smaller. Aerial reconnaissance has, over the past two decades, revealed a number of relatively small temporary camps ranging in size from about 5.0 to 15.0 hectares, in the lands between Forth and Tay (Table 2). Even the smallest of these could have accommodated several thousand legionary troops together with their *impedimenta* –

Table 2

POSSIBLE FLAVIAN MARCHING-CAMPS IN THE PRESUMED AREA OF
AGRICOLA'S SIXTH CAMPAIGN

			Area
A.	*Stracathro-type gates*	Bochastle	19.8ha
		Dalginross I	9.5ha
		Lochlands I	<9.7ha
		Malling I	10.4ha
B.	*Plain clavicular gates*	Lochlands II	<5.2ha
C.	*'33-acre' group*	Ardoch II	12.1ha
	non-clavicular	Bonnytown	c.14.1ha(?)
		Dornock	9.6ha
		Dunblane I	12.0ha
		Lochlands III	c.14.8ha(?)
		Mains of Strageath	13.5ha
D.	*'11–15 acres'*	Ardoch I	5.4ha
	non-clavicular	Ardoch III	4.5ha
		Dalginross II	<3.6ha
		Dunblane II	5.0ha
		Lochlands IV	c.5.6ha
		Malling II	5.0ha
		Ochtertyre	<6.0ha

the baggage train which accompanied the columns of the Roman army on the march – as well as a number of auxiliaries. Although it has been suggested (St Joseph 1969, 114) that some of these sites belong to the Agricolan phase of conquest, the assumption has been seriously questioned (Hanson 1978, 144–5; 1987, 126–7). It is extremely interesting, therefore, that many of the temporary camps in figure 5 could be seen as playing a role in just such a scenario. In the early summer, Agricola moved north of the isthmus. The main collecting-ground for such an operation appears to have been the extensive sand-and-gravel plateau to the north-west of Camelon, where at least twelve temporary camps have so far been identified by aerial survey; the resulting complex is comparable in form and purpose with that located at Newstead on the Tweed. Recent discoveries and re-examination of air photograph evidence at

Lochlands on the north-western fringes of this area (Maxwell and Wilson 1987, 29–30, 32, 39) have not only revealed a camp with Stracathro-type gates, at least 9.7 hectares in size, intersecting another with *claviculae*, but have also necessitated the re-interpretation of cropmarks previously taken to define a single 17-hectare camp; the latter now appears likely to form parts of at least two and possibly as many as five or six separate camps, between 5 and 15 hectares in area, which respect the former sites and possess gates that were defended by *titula*. From the presence of Stracathro-type camps at Malling, Bochastle and Dalginross, one would presume that Agricola's army was already operating in relatively small groups, one party being detailed to comb the head-waters of the rivers Teith and Forth; the other parties may have had orders to cross the Teith – possibly near Ochtertyre where the camp of Craigarnhall, on the opposite bank, marks Severus' presumed crossing-point, but more probably near the newly discovered fort at Doune – and then proceed north through Strathallan, one party then turning eastwards into Fife while the other pushed on to the Earn. At what stage Agricola learned of the Caledonian invasion-threat cannot be determined; however, his intention may have been to hold, or at least patrol, the line of the Earn from where it issues from the hills at Comrie to its very mouth, the assumption being that the enemy would cross the Tay above its confluence with that river.

It is impossible to say where the night battle took place or which camps held the beleaguered and relieving party. Three categories, or possibly four, can be made out: the very largest is represented by Bochastle, which is closely comparable in size with the camp that predates the legionary fortress at Inchtuthil; the second comprises about five sites *c.* 13.4 hectares in average area; the third consists of a similar number, approaching 10 hectares in area, some with Stracathro-type or plain clavicular gates, others with *titula* (figure 4); and finally a group of much smaller camps, ranging from about 4.5 to 5.6 hectares in size, only one of which appears to be of Stracathro type. It would be tempting to identify the last group, capable of accommodating a mixed force of legionaries and auxiliaries at the very least 3,500 strong, with the bivouacs of the Ninth Legion as it moved up from Ochtertyre through Strathallan to Strathearn, now re-using the camps of units that had preceded it, now riding 'point', with its colleagues in its wake. Thus it may have been somewhere in the broad valley of the Earn that the Caledonian forces massed to break through the Roman 'line' at its weakest point. To do so they would have had to pass across the front of one or other of the larger battle-groups, and it was presumably in the course of this lateral movement that Agricola's scouts, operating well in advance of the main body, picked up their tracks. The rest is, literally, history.

Such a reconstruction of events is, of course, purely hypothetical, but the rarity of the smaller class of camps to the north and east of the Tay strongly suggests that these areas were not the scene of the probing operations assigned by Tacitus to the sixth campaign. Even if that assumption is wrong and the attack on the Ninth Legion took place deeper in Caledonia, the very extent and character of the territory lying between the Trossachs and the East Neuk of Fife, together with what we have seen of the political complexity of the area, make it most improbable, especially after such an equivocal victory, that Agricola would have had the time or the audacity to do more than confirm his grasp on the land that had been overrun in the earlier part of the season. The two sides had nevertheless measured the length of each other's swords, and both had realised that nothing less than a pitched battle could decide the issue; rightly or wrongly, they believed the victors would be masters of Caledonia.

THREE

The Battle for Caledonia

AFTER describing the varying fortunes of the sixth campaign, Tacitus offers an account of the mutiny of the Usipi (*Agricola*, xxviii), a cohort of German tribesmen recruited into the *auxilia*, who had been brought to Britain for their military training. The reason for the insertion of this anecdote was doubtless two-fold: to describe a remarkable incident that occurred during Agricola's governorship, and to allow the tension of the narrative to be relaxed before the reader was exposed to the crescendo of the final act. Once again Tacitus, the master of effect, is preparing his audience to accept a particular version of historical events. Appropriately, the opening passage is presented in sombre colours.

Agricola, 29: At the beginning of the summer Agricola was dealt a personal blow when he lost his son, who had been born the previous year. This calamity he bore not with ostentatious fortitude, as the majority of men of action might; on the other hand, he did not give way to tears and womanly lamentation, but though he grieved, he sought remedies for his grief, and one of them was war.

Accordingly, he despatched the fleet to harry the enemy generally, so spreading extensive doubt and panic, while the army, operating without its usual baggage-train, was strengthened by the addition of the bravest of the British auxiliary units, whose loyalty had been tried through long years of peace; thus Agricola came at last to *Mons Graupius*, which the enemy had made their base. For the British tribes had in no sense been broken by the result of the previous year's conflict and now looked to receive nothing but retribution or slavery. Moreover, at long last they had learned that a common alliance was the only way to ward off a common danger, and by invoking pacts or by diplomatic negotiations had brought out the armed might of all the Caledonian tribes.

Already 30,000 warriors might be seen, and there was still a steady stream of recruits coming in – young men in their prime and older men still hale and full of vigour, each one with a glorious reputation in battle and wearing the badges of honour he had won – when one of their leaders, a man of outstanding courage and lofty lineage, who was called Calgacus, is reputed to have addressed this speech to the assembled host as they clamoured for battle:

Agricola, 30: 'Whenever I consider the origin of this conflict and our present peril, I am convinced that your unanimity today will prove to be the beginning of the liberation of the whole of Britain. For you are all united, without a taint of servile compulsion, and there are no lands beyond us to which we may flee; not even the sea can offer safety while the Roman fleet is there to threaten us. So it has come to armed conflict, the honourable path for men of valour and likewise the safest refuge even for weaker spirits. All earlier combatants, who strove against the Romans with varying degrees of success, could expect to see their fortunes retrieved by our exertions. For we are the noblest of all the peoples of Britain and therefore dwell in its inmost sanctuary. We look out on no realms of slavery, our eyes still unpolluted by the touch of tyranny. This secluded land of ours, steeped in fable, has preserved us for this day. But now the furthest bounds of Britain have been laid bare and even the mystery of our isolation only whets the appetite of the invader. There are no tribes beyond to help us, nothing but bare rocks, the cruel sea – and worse than these, the Romans, whose arrogance you will try in vain to escape, whether by compliance or good behaviour. These men have pillaged the whole world, and, now that their career of universal ruin has exhausted the resources of the land, they take a toothcomb to the sea. If their enemies are wealthy, they indulge their greed, if poor, their lust for glory; neither the East nor the West contains enough to satisfy them. Alone of mortals they lust after affluence and poverty with equal appetite. Robbery, butchery, pillage – these are what they mean when they talk of "Empire", and "Peace" is the word they use when all that is left is desolation . . .'

Agricola, 32: 'Don't let the glitter or the display of insubstantial gold and silver trappings dismay you; it will afford the enemy no protection and cannot hurt you. There, in the enemy's own line of battle, we shall find hands to fight for us: the British troops will see that our cause is their own; the Gauls will remember the liberty they have lost, and the rest of their German levies will desert them, just as in the recent mutiny of the Usipi. And when we have finished with this rabble there is nothing more to fear, just empty forts, settlements of ageing veterans, and enfeebled townships, with unscrupulous officials and rebellious citizens locked in strife. On this side you have your country's leader and a free army, on that side taxes, forced labour in the mines, and the entire catalogue of servile punishment; the issue of this battle will decide whether you submit to them for the rest of time or make them here and now the objects of your wrath. And so, as you move forward to the fight, remember your ancestors and have a thought for those who will come after you.'

Agricola, 33: This speech galvanised the enemy, as is the way with barbarians, into an uproar of war-whoops and raucous shouting. And now the enemy battalions began to move, and the sunlight glinted on brandished steel as the bolder spirits broke out in front of the rest; and their troops were actually being drawn up in line of battle, when Agricola began to address his men – they were in excellent spirits and scarcely to be kept within the confines of the camp, but he reckoned they needed to be roused even further.

'Comrades in arms, this is now the seventh year that you have been engaged upon the conquest of Britannia, in the glorious name of the Roman empire, and through the honest toil of every one of us. Never once in the course of so many campaigns and battles, whether we had to display courage against the enemy or endure patient toiling against Nature herself, have I had regrets about my troops, nor have you about your general. And so together we have surpassed the limits of conquest reached by previous governors and earlier armies; our grasp of the furthest limit of Britain is not vain and fanciful, but real, by means of armed occupation. Britain has now been truly discovered and subdued. So many times on the march, when you were toiling through swamps and labouring across mountain-ranges and rivers, I would hear the bravest of you ask "When do we get a sight of the enemy? When will they come to grips with us?" Well, now they are coming; they have been flushed from their dens, and your prayers and courage will have an open field. Every circumstance will combine to magnify a victory, but if you lose, they will work against you; for while we are advancing it is a splendid, noble achievement to have marched so great a distance, to have come through forests and crossed firths, but if we have to retreat, then all these things which now signal our success will then be fraught with danger. For we do not know the country as the enemy knows it, nor are we blessed with the same ample supply of food; all we have is our weapons in our hands, and on these everything must depend.

'As far as I am concerned, I came to realise long since that an army's rear is never safe, nor is a general's. So be prepared to die with honour, for it is better than living in disgrace, and it may be you will find that the paths of glory lead also to salvation. It will be no disgrace to have perished at the very limit of the natural world!

Agricola, 34: 'If these had been strange and unknown tribes ranged in battle against us, I should encourage you with the examples of other armies. But as it is, just tell over your own battle-honours and question the evidence of your own eyes. These are the men whom last year you swept from the field of battle with a shout, when they had fallen upon a single legion, with all the stealth of a night attack. These men are the men who hold the British all-comer's record for running – from the enemy – and that is why they have survived so long. Just as all the bravest animals would burst out at you when you made your way through forests and glens, but the timid and slothful were driven off by the mere sound of your column on the march, even so the fiercest of the Britons have long since fallen, and all that is left is a pack of craven cowards. Now that you have at last found them, it does not mean they have decided to make a stand; they have just been overtaken. The extremity of their situation and the numbing influence of sheer terror have riveted their battalions to the ground where they stand, and it is there that you are fated to provide the spectacle of a great and glorious victory.

'Have done with frontier wars in Britain, and make this day the glorious crown of fifty years' campaigning. Prove to your countrymen that, wherever the blame lies for never-ending warfare and civil unrest, it is certainly not with the soldiers of their provincial armies!'

Agricola, 35: Even while Agricola was speaking, the troops' enthusiasm would burst forth, and the conclusion of the address was followed by intense activity as everyone immediately rushed to arm themselves. While they were seized by this ferment of eagerness Agricola assigned them their fighting positions: the auxiliary infantry, 8,000 strong, made a strong centre to the line and 3,000 cavalry were spread out on the wings; behind them stood the legionary detachments, just in front of the marching-camp – for it would be a glorious thing if the battle could be won without a single drop of Roman blood spilt, but they were to act as a reserve should the auxiliaries be driven back.

The British forces had occupied the heights for the two-fold purpose of making a brave show and overawing our men, with the result that their front line was drawn up at the far edge of the level ground between the two armies and the others, as though linked together in a solid mass, towered over them, all the way up the slope of the hill. Meanwhile, enemy chariots careered across the intervening plain in noisy sallies.

At this point Agricola began to be afraid that the enemy would use their superior strength to launch simultaneous attacks on our centre and flanks, so he extended his lines, although it meant that the army would be rather thinly spread and many of his staff advised him to bring up the legions. But being more sanguine in his expectations, and quite resolute in the face of difficulties, he dismounted from his horse, and took up a position in front of the standards.

Agricola, 36: At the beginning of the engagement, the battle was joined at long range. The Britons used their huge swords and little shields with skill and pertinacity to parry or ward off the missiles hurled at them by our troops, and themselves poured down a really heavy barrage; finally Agricola encouraged four cohorts of Batavians and two cohorts of Tungrians to come to close quarters, a form of battle in which our men had a long history of military training but which proved awkward to the enemy since they had such massive swords to wield and only flimsy shields to protect them. For the Briton's swords were designed for slashing and had no point and hence they were of little use when it came to a grapple in close-quarter fighting. Consequently, as the Batavians went to it in a flurry of blows, slamming into the enemy with the bosses of their shields and stabbing at their faces, they overcame the warriors who had been stationed at the bottom of the slope and began to advance uphill; and the other cohorts, inspired by their example, pressed home their attacks and cut down the troops opposite to them; many were left only half slain, some even unwounded, as the tide of battle swept swiftly by.

Meanwhile certain cavalry troops had begun to take part in the battle which had hitherto involved only infantry – (the chariots they had been opposing were now in flight) – but although at first they had increased the enemy panic, their attack had now ground to a halt as the hill got steeper and the ranks of the enemy more densely packed. It was certainly not a typical cavalry engagement, with the Roman troops finding it difficult to keep their footing on the sloping ground and being jostled at the same time by the cavalry mounts. In addition, there were the stray chariots and riderless horses, which careered about wherever panic drove them, coming at our troops from the flanks or even head-on.

Agricola, 37: Those British forces who had so far taken no part in the fighting, but had remained on the high ground, idly scorning the weakness of our army, gradually began to descend and would have worked their way round to the rear of our victorious auxiliaries had not Agricola, who had been afraid of this very eventuality, despatched four regiments of cavalry from the emergency reserve to check their attack. The fierceness of the

enemy assault was, however, equalled by the sharpness of the re-
pulse with which they were sent packing. Thus the Caledonians'
stratagem was turned against them, for the cavalry was detailed
by Agricola to desist from its frontal attack and fall upon the
main mass of the enemy from the rear. Then indeed, far and
wide across the battlefield, there were scenes of frightful
savagery; the Roman forces in pursuit, wounding or taking
prisoners, only to slaughter them when others came their way.
The behaviour of the individual soldiers of the Caledonian army
was now dictated by their own character or inclination: whole
companies turned tail when pursued by a mere handful, while
others, although unarmed, freely sought death in suicidal
attacks. Everywhere you looked there were corpses and weapons,
mangled limbs and blood-soaked ground. Occasionally, even
among the defeated Britons there were instances of enraged
bravery; for as the fighting got nearer to the woods, the enemy
banded together and used their knowledge of the terrain to
encircle those of our men who were recklessly leading the
pursuit. Appreciable losses would have been sustained because
of this over-confidence had not Agricola, who was bustling about
all over the battlefield, given orders to deal with the situation:
the powerful light infantry were to flush out the enemy, like
beaters; where the forest was denser, some of the cavalry were to
dismount and where it was more open the rest were to sweep
through it. However, when the enemy saw that the pursuit had
been resumed with the troops deployed in regular order, they
once more fled, not in companies as before, nor watching out for
each other, but, scattered and avoiding contact with their
comrades, they made for the remotest wilderness. The pursuit
ended only when night fell and everyone had had enough.
Around ten thousand of the enemy were slain, while our
casualties numbered only three hundred and sixty, among whom
was Aulus Atticus, the commander of an auxiliary unit, who was
borne off into the midst of the enemy by youthful zeal and the
mettle of his charger.

Agricola, 38: What with the rejoicing and the booty, it was a
happy night for the victorious army. The Britons, on the other

hand, dispersed, and the voices of both men and women were
raised in lamentation; they carried off the wounded and called
out for survivors; they abandoned their homes and burned them
in a fit of rage, sought out hiding-places and straightaway left
them, formed some sort of concerted plan and then split up.
Sometimes they were crushed by the mere sight of their families,
but more often they were driven wild. It was reliably reported
that some actually killed their wives and children, seemingly in
pity.

The light of day revealed more widely the spectacle of victory;
everywhere there was a great silence; the hills were deserted and
in the distance columns of smoke rose from the burning
buildings, but our scouts came across no one in their reconnaissance. And when the patrols that had been sent out in all
directions reported only confused signs of flight with no evidence
anywhere that the enemy was regrouping, Agricola led the army
towards the coast and the lands of the Boresti, for the season was
already spent and it was impossible to campaign further.
Arriving at the coast, he received hostages and instructed the
commander of the fleet to sail around Britain, giving him
appropriate reinforcements, although the news of the victory
spread sufficient panic before the fleet to make it unnecessary.
Agricola himself led the infantry and cavalry back into winter
quarters, moving in easy stages so that the spirits of these newly
conquered peoples should be shaken by the leisurely nature of
his progress.

About the same time, in favourable weather and attended by
glowing reports of its achievement, the fleet reached the
Trucculensian harbour, from which it had returned in its entirety
having sailed along the nearer coast of Britain.

Agricola, 39: Domitian received an account of all these
happenings, as was his custom, with an expression of joy but
with a troubled breast, even although Agricola had not sought to
inflate his achievements with boastful dispatches; for the
emperor was well aware that the triumph he had recently
celebrated for his own German campaign had been a farce, with
slaves acquired in the market-place made up to look like
prisoners of war with suitable clothes and dyed hair . . .

So runs the account that Tacitus gives of the battle at Mons Graupius. Before discussing the conflict in detail, however, it may be helpful to examine the evidence presented in the text for the timing and context of the victory, and to consider a little of the archaeological background.

It is a pity that Tacitus' preoccupation with the battle itself prevented him from providing more information about the developments which led up to it. It would seem (see below, p. 115) that the action took place later in the year than any of Agricola's other British exploits, apart from that of the first year, when operations were delayed by his late arrival in the province (xviii). We cannot be sure why this was so. All that we are told, or rather the way in which we are told it, prompts us to believe that the event which took place in the early part of the campaigning season, the death of Agricola's infant son, had delayed the start of operations. On the human level this is quite credible, but we need not imagine that a provincial governor could have allowed domestic matters to regulate his official life entirely. Of more basic relevance was the need to amass a field army of suitable strength, for it was clear that a head-on collision between the two sides was the objective that each had in mind, and reports of enemy concentration coming in from the north probably left Agricola in no doubt that a maximum effort would be required. Tacitus' remarks about the inclusion of British *auxilia* in the force may be an implied acknowledgement that military resources were severely strained. Certainly it was a calculated risk to incorporate elements who might transfer their loyalty if they saw the enemy star in the ascendant, and the fact that Tacitus represented the Caledonian leader prophesying such mutiny in his battle-field address (xxxii, 3) strongly suggests that both commanders knew it was not impossible. We learn in the account of the battle itself (xxxv, 2; xxxvii, 1) that Agricola's auxiliary strength included 8,000 infantry and at least 3,000, probably 5,000, horse; the legionary complement is not specified, but it is unlikely to have outnumbered the *auxilia* and was probably somewhat weaker, say 10,000–12,000 troops, the whole army thus amounting to not much more than 27,000.

The gathering together of such a force and its assembling at some suitable campaign base, appropriately equipped and instructed for a decisive battle, would not have been achieved without considerable planning and organisational activity, but it is passed over by Tacitus without comment, while the momentous march to the battlefield from the start-line is subsumed in the single phrase *ad montem Graupium pervenit* ('he came to the Graupian mount'). The information that the army was *expeditus*, 'travelling light, without baggage train', might tell us anything: that the emphasis was on speed, that Agricola envisaged no lengthy operations requiring artillery, or that the target was relatively close at hand; it could also mean that Agricola was intending to operate in rough terrain or ill-drained country, where a baggage train would have been a considerable hindrance (cf. Tac. *Hist*. iii, 51). According to Tacitus (xxxii, 5), on the eve of the battle the Roman army was comparatively short of supplies and it is improbable that Agricola would have ventured into enemy territory in such conditions had it not been possible to extricate his army within a reasonably short period. On the other hand, there may have been plans to pick up supplies from the fleet or, since the campaign evidently took place at the end of the summer, to forage amongst native cornfields. The latter possibility is by no means as unlikely as was once thought (Piggott 1958, 19–27), but even if one allows the existence of a relatively advanced rural economy in north-east Scotland at this period, it is improbable that supplies could have been obtained in sufficient quantities by this method at any given point on the march; the scale of the problem also argues against supply by sea over a protracted campaign.

The question of how far the army had to march is really two questions: where did it start from, and where did it fight? Most modern archaeologists and historians would concur in supposing that the answer to the first was the line of the Tay, a proposition that has won general acceptance since Macdonald's statement (1919, 115) that 'Inchtuthil marks a stage of some moment in the pursuit of *Mons Graupius*', although few, if any, now believe that it served even as a semi-permanent base in that campaign. What we have seen of the archaeological evidence relating to contemporary native society, in the context of the sixth campaign (pp. 27–9), reinforces such a view. It remains to be seen if similar evidence casts any light on the operations of Agricola's seventh season.

To a certain extent, the same evidence may be adduced, in that it

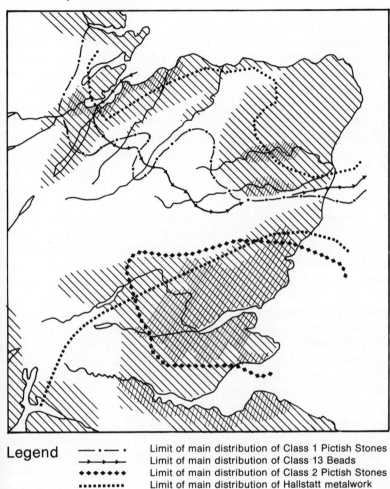

Legend

— · — ·   Limit of main distribution of Class 1 Pictish Stones
→—→—→   Limit of main distribution of Class 13 Beads
♦♦♦♦♦♦♦   Limit of main distribution of Class 2 Pictish Stones
▪▪▪▪▪▪▪▪▪   Limit of main distribution of Hallstatt metalwork
••••••••••   Limit of main distribution of Covesea metalwork

Figure 6. Density of distribution of Iron Age structures between the Moray Firth and the Forth (densest areas cross-hatched) with evidence of continuing exclusivity of artefact distribution North and South of the Mounth.

gives good reasons for believing that the Caledonian peoples who were the focus of Agricola's attention in the final campaign were bounded on the south-west by the upper and middle reaches of the Tay. However, the literary sources, particularly those of the later Roman period, emphasise that these peoples formed a confederacy comprising two basic groups: in Ptolemy they appear as the *Taexali* and *Vacomagi*, who inhabited those areas of north-eastern Scotland lying respectively to the north and south of the Mounth (figures 6 and 9). Although it is impossible to draw a precise boundary between these two tribal groups, it cannot fail to be noticed that from the Neolithic period (as shown by the concentrative distribution of carved stone balls) to the late Bronze Age (as shown by the respective distribution patterns of Covesea and Hallstatt metalwork) the areas of Strathmore and Buchan drew upon different cultural traditions (figure 6). As the same territorial exclusivity is displayed more than a millennium later by the distribution of Pictish Symbol-stones of classes I and II, it would be natural to assume that this artefactual evidence bears witness to a political or cultural cleavage of some permanence, which also existed in the Roman Iron Age. And, indeed, the clustering of examples of such roughly contemporary objects as the massive 'Donside' terrets, or glass beads of class 13 and 14 (Guido 1978, 85–9; figure 6), appears to confirm that the situation could have been of very real significance to Agricola in his final campaign; it may be helpful, therefore, to give a brief description of the geography of the probable theatre of operations.

The southernmost portion is divided into three or four separate zones: *1*) the broad valley of Strathmore, delimited on the north-west by the foothills of the Grampian massif and on the south-east by the Sidlaws and lesser outcrops; *2*) a coastal plain of varying width; and *3*) the Howe of the Mearns, a north-eastwards continuation of Strathmore, extending from the North Esk to the Bervie Water, where the Grampians and coastal hills unite in a rolling plateau, and the north-faring traveller finds himself edged closer and closer to the sea. The face of the Grampian wall is breached at intervals by several rivers: in its south-western half by tributaries of the Tay – the Ericht and the Isla; to the north-east by such as the Prosen Water, the West Water, and the North and South Esk, which wind across the broad levels of the Strath and eventually fall into the sea at or near

Figure 7. Air photograph of Iron Age unenclosed settlement at Kirktonbarns, Fife; cropmarks reveal the sunken circular and annular floors of individual timber houses.

Montrose. These and their tributaries could have presented obstacles of differing size to an army on the march; and in Roman times there would also have been vast areas of morass to negotiate, particularly in the vicinity of Forfar and to the south-west of Fordoun, where nowadays, after centuries of improvement, there lie extensive tracts of agricultural land.

Beyond Stonehaven the character of the country changes. The landscape opens up towards the north, where the gently rolling plains of Buchan extend to the rocky headland of Kinnaird Head, Ptolemy's *Taexalorum Promontorium*; but first the lower reaches of the rivers Dee and Don must be crossed, the former a formidable obstacle. For the traveller heading towards the coast of the Moray Firth and the richer farmlands of the Laich of Moray or Nairn a north-westerly course must be pursued along the valley of the Urie and thence across the uplands of Strathbogie to cross the River Deveron at or below Huntly. Beyond this, the Pass of Grange and the valley of the River Isla offer a relatively direct route between the Aultmore Hills and the northern skirts of the Grampians to Strathspey. Across the Spey a succession of ridge-routes leads westwards, without major hindrance, past Elgin, Forres and Nairn to the head of the Great Glen.

The modern traveller, consulting his map as he follows a course through the country just described, from the Tay to the shores of the Moray Firth, will find that at several points the hills that overlook his route are crowned with the remains of ancient fortifications. Many of them are particularly well-preserved or impressive and hold an honoured place in archaeological literature: Finavon, Barry Hill, Turin Hill and the Brown and White Caterthuns in Angus, for example; or Barmekin of Echt, Mither Tap of Bennachie, and Dunnideer of Insch in Aberdeenshire. Yet, pleasing though it might be to imagine the Roman columns making their way beneath the frowning ramparts of these multivallate strongholds, there is every reason to believe that most belong to a much earlier phase of the Iron Age and would have long ceased to present a military threat to an invading army; the rest are as likely to have been the fortified centres of the post-Roman period.

Although the quantity and quality of evidence is simply not sufficient to provide a detailed and accurate picture of the way of life of the peoples of Caledonia, it would be reasonable to presume that, in the main, like the Picts who succeeded them, they were essentially 'simple, peaceful farmers' (Alcock 1980, 86), albeit farmers in a typically strife-torn Celtic society (cf. Rankin 1987 passim); they lived for the most part in scattered, open villages of no great size, or relatively small homesteads and enclosures; the archaeological traces of these habitations, comprising round timber and stone-founded houses up to 18 metres in diameter and the enigmatic underground structures known as souterrains, have been identified throughout all

Figure 8. Air photograph of souterrain at Burnhead of Auchterhouse, Tayside; ripening barley above the revetting walls of the souterrain-passage outlines the underground structure with perfect clarity.

parts of Caledonia (figures 7 and 8), although excavation has still to indicate their precise nature and the length of the period over which they were in use. Equally important matters, such as the apparent absence of the hierarchy of sites so prevalent in south-eastern Scotland, and there interpreted, wrongly or rightly, as an indication of increasingly complex social structure, also wait to be considered in the light of the knowledge newly acquired by aerial and terrestrial fieldwork. Nevertheless, even in its very crudest state, such evidence demonstrates that, far from being primeval forest, much of north-eastern Scotland in the time of Agricola was a 'managed' landscape, whether used for tillage or pastoralism, involving the careful control of both upland and lowland areas for the good of the community. The Roman army's sudden irruption into this peaceful scene, threatening

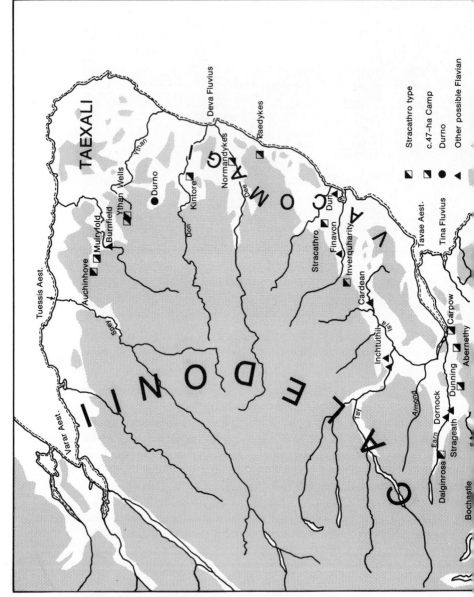

Figure 9. Roman military installations probably associated with the final Agricolan campaigns. (Land over 200 m OD shaded.)

the economic and political equilibrium of an ordered society enjoying the closest of links with its territory, namely that of guardian and husbandman, is an easily comprehensible explanation of the ferocity with which that society united in armed resistance. More than half a millennium later the Pictish peoples, enjoying, it would seem, a similar social structure, were capable of equally ferocious reaction to the threat of invasion.

The evidence for Roman military activity in this area comprises two basic categories of structure, permanent fortified sites and temporary camps. In modern times, thanks mainly to the aerial reconnaissance programme conducted on behalf of the Cambridge University Committee for Aerial Photography under the direction of Professor J. K. S. St Joseph with the assistance of D. R. Wilson, our knowledge of the latter category is much improved. (Indeed, it would be difficult to exaggerate the importance of the role played by aerial survey in the increase of our knowledge about this aspect of Roman Scotland; cf. St Joseph 1976; Maxwell and Wilson 1987, 29–41.) But air photograph evidence is seldom as explicit as we would like, and the assignment of any camp to a particular period of Roman conquest can seldom be supported by anything more explicit than morphology, or its observed structural relationship to another (undated) temporary site.

In Scotland north of the Tay there are five separate categories of Roman temporary camps, large enough to have accommodated an invading army or one of its component elements. Two of these categories, comprising camps that measure 25 and 52 hectares respectively in average size, have been provisionally dated to the early third century AD; they are assumed to represent the operations in successive years of the Emperor Septimius Severus and his sons as they sought to bring to heel the fractious Caledonians and Maeatae (St Joseph 1969, 114–19; 1973, 230–3). The distribution of these camps indicates the progress of armies at the rate of 10–25 kilometres per day from the Forth-Clyde isthmus to the north-eastern end of Strathmore and the Bervie Water, as well as in eastern Fife and the coastal tract of Angus; the close correspondence of this distribution with that of unenclosed native settlements and souterrains is noteworthy, and probably not a mere coincidence.

For many years it was thought that the distribution of the 52-

Table 3

POSSIBLE AGRICOLAN MARCHING-CAMPS IN NORTH-EAST SCOTLAND

Type A	Site	Area
large	Raedykes	37.6ha
(gates with *titula*)	Normandykes	c.43.0ha
	Kintore	44.5ha
	Ythan Wells	44.9ha
	Muiryfold	44.1ha
	Logie Durno	58.3ha
Type B		
'Stracathro'	Stracathro	15.8ha
gates	Ythan Wells	14.1ha
	Auchinhove	>12.0ha
Other		
(non-clavicular gates)	Finavon	15.0ha
	Cardean	>13.5ha
	Burnfield	> 8.0ha

hectare group extended to the north of the Mounth, but St Joseph (1973, 231–3) has pointed out that the camps in this area are appreciably smaller and probably formed a distinct category whose members actually averaged about 44 hectares in area, although one, Raedykes near Stonehaven, was only 38 hectares. This group (figure 10, Table 3) also indicated the line of march of an army of considerable size, travelling from 10 to 22 kilometres each day (figures 9 and 24) as it proceeded from the Mounth north-westwards towards Strathbogie, skirting the edge of the Grampian massif. It has also been suggested (St Joseph 1978a and below, pp. 104–8) that a camp of c.58 hectares situated at Durno, roughly midway between the camps of Ythan Wells and Kintore, should be included in the same group, and despite its difference in size, the similarity in the disposition and form of its gateway would support such a classification. But there is an equally close similarity between Durno and camps of the 52-hectare group, which are assumed to be Severan, while the only two sites of comparable size to be securely dated to the Flavian period (Dunning and Abernethy) are both significantly less elongated (cf. Maxwell 1980, 28–9). Relative dating of the 44-hectare camps has been

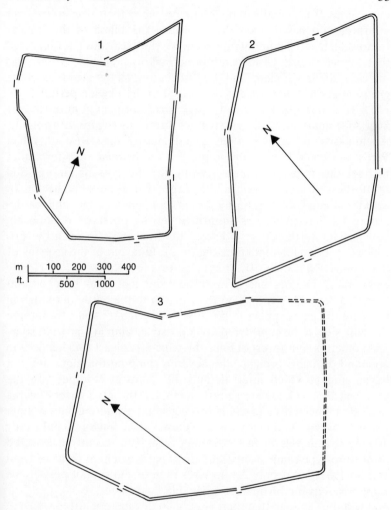

Figure 10. Plans of examples of probable Agricolan marching camps in the North: 1, Raedykes; 2, Ythan Wells; 3, Durno.

obtained at one site, Ythan Wells, where excavation showed (St Joseph 1969, 112) that it overlay a camp of 14 hectares whose gates were of the Stracathro type. Although the interval separating these two camps was initially thought to be more than a century – an interpretation based upon the nature of the filling of the smaller camp's ditch at the point of intersection – the excavator later reported that a much shorter period was not necessarily precluded. If that was the case, the larger camp and, by association, all the members of the group might also have been constructed in the Flavian period.

There is one other relatively large Stracathro camp in north-east Scotland, apart from the eponymous site itself (figure 9, Table 3); Auchinhove, which lies about 23 kilometres north-west of Ythan Wells and could conceivably represent the bivouac of a force that had set out from that camp heading for the Pass of Grange and Strathspey. Stracathro, only a little larger than either (15.8 hectares), could, but need not necessarily, have accommodated the same battle-group; its Flavian date is confirmed by the observed relationship between its north-eastern side and the annexe of the nearby fort, which it presumably underlies (figure 2). Finavon, at the crossing of the South Esk some 30 kilometres to the south-west, is closely comparable in area and proportions and may also have accommodated Agricola's troops on their march to the battle, although in this case the gates appear to be defended by *titula*. Apart from these the only sites to be considered are a possible camp at Cardean, some 38 kilometres south-west of Finavon, which is at least 13.5 hectares in area and probably predates the Severan camp on the same site, but by an undetermined interval, and the camp at Burnfield on the Deveron about 7 kilometres north of Huntly; the latter covers an area of at least 8 hectares and would make a suitable intermediate resting-place between Auchinhove and Ythan Wells, but one could only assume that it was in fact contemporary. The recently discovered Stracathro-type camp at Inverquharity near Kirriemuir (Maxwell and Wilson 1987, 16) is only 2.4 hectares in area and cannot possibly be categorised as the bivouac of a sizeable field-force.

It will thus be seen that there is enough raw material from which to fashion a hypothetical northward march for field-forces of widely differing strength, ranging possibly from 16,000 to 60,000 strong; in recent years several scholars have ventured to employ them in discussions of the final Agricolan campaign; with what success will be considered later (pp. 94, 98 and 104), for it is now time to turn to the actual battle.

It is ironic that although Tacitus has taken the trouble to identify the site of the battle by name, we are not thereby enlightened about its location. The modern name 'Grampian' applied to the main upland massif of northern Britain itself is no guide, either philologically or geographically, to the original feature; the former derives form the printed version 'Grampius' which appears in the *editio princeps* (Puteolanus) produced by Francisco dal Pozzo in Milan a little before 1480. It would appear that the original Latinised name was nearer to *Craupius* (cf. Rivet and Smith 1979, 370–1) and this may possibly be derived from an original Celtic form **Craup* related to modern Welsh *crwb* 'a hump'. Although this is an attractive solution, derivation from the variant **graup*, related to Greek γρυπός, has also been suggested, which might indicate a physical feature that was altogether more prominent. It would be a gross oversimplification of the problem to say that the choice lay between 'hill of the hump' or 'hill of the peak', and even were it not, who can tell precisely what form of hill or mountain either phrase might aptly describe? This alone can be allowed, that, with relation to the battlefield, the hill must have appeared so imposing a feature that it was natural for it to give its name to the conflict, but there can be no indication in the name alone of its absolute scale, and in the event scholars have not hesitated to identify it with features of widely differing size (pp. 101 and 104). The possibility that the textual tradition may be grossly corrupt has never seriously been considered, but one is tempted to wonder if the Puteolanus variant *grampium* is not worthy of closer examination. Palaeographically viewed, it is close enough to *quempiam* which could be interpreted as a copyist's substitute for an unrecognisably mis-spelt original, perhaps influenced by the words *quem iam* following shortly after. It would be pleasing, if fanciful, to think that a range of mountains and, nowadays, a local government region were named after 'Mount Something-or-other!'

There is however no dispute about the etymology of the name given by Tacitus to the person selected by the Caledonians as their leader. *Calgacus*, which is related to Irish *calgach*, means 'swordsman', but whether this was a title conferred upon the elected leader of the northern host, or his given name, is unknown. Tacitus later mentions the Caledonian warriors wielding long swords in battle as though these were exceptional items of equipment and it is possible that, like the claymore of later centuries, the sword was the Caledonian weapon *par excellence*, and both primacy and prowess in war were equated with pre-eminence in swordplay.

Tacitus' account of the actual encounter between the Roman and Caledonian armies suggests that after both sides had arrived at Mons Graupius there were seven separate stages: the leaders' speeches; the ordering of the battle-lines and preliminary skirmishing; the exchange of missiles; a close-quarter engagement involving both infantry and mounted troops; a Caledonian attempt to outflank the Roman line and Agricola's countercheck; a Roman cavalry attack on the Caledonian flank and rear; and finally the rout of the Caledonian forces.

(i) *The Speeches*

Although the highly polished rhetorical exercises presented by Tacitus can bear little relation to speeches that were actually delivered, they form an important part of the narrative, for two basic reasons: firstly, it is extremely likely that some words of exhortation and counsel were in fact addressed to each army by its commander, and secondly, presentation of the speeches in a literary form allowed Tacitus to introduce ideas and details about the context of the struggle in a singularly imposing fashion without appearing to sacrifice the objectivity of a reporter. Thus, much of each address is the staple of every eve-of-battle speech from the dawn of history: William of Poitiers credited William the Conqueror with similar remarks before Hastings – victory would be the reward for courage, retreat in an unknown country would be fatal, the enemy had been beaten before – the sort of things a soldier needs to know and hear from his commander. Interspersed with such routine encouragement, however, are topics which provide useful background 'colour'. Calgacus reminds his men and us: that the 'remoteness' factor may work against them by adding to the lustre of a Roman victory; that Agricola and the Roman army in its isolated position ran the same risks as Suetonius Paullinus when overreaching himself on the eve of the Boudiccan rising; that there was a real chance of Agricola's army disintegrating if the auxiliaries were to seek their freedom as the Batavian cohorts had done just over a dozen years before. It may be

Figure 11. An antiquarian view of the conflict at Mons Graupius; Calgacus rallies the troops.

that the insertion of such ideas sprang from the picture that Tacitus had formed of the real situation, as described by Agricola personally, but which he felt disinclined to mention as part of the historical narrative because it might suggest a lack of prudence on the part of the former governor. Be that as it may, there can be no doubt that the speeches have impressed generations of readers by both their elegance and the nobility of sentiment. Indeed, one edition of the *Agricola* (Smith 1828, 172–83) contains a translation of the entire speech of Calgacus into Gaelic; it was produced by the Celtic philologist, Dr W. Shaw, who was convinced that a report of the words actually uttered 'had been procured by Agricola, from some Roman prisoners . . . in the Caledonian camp, and recovered after the battle'!

(ii) *Deployment of Troops*
The speeches done, the armies faced each other for their grim purpose. The majority of the 30,000 credited by Tacitus to the Caledonians were foot-soldiers, who sensibly maintained the advantage conferred by their position on *Mons Graupius*, only the foremost line of battle being drawn up on on the same level as the Roman troops; the rest were packed in serried ranks on the slope that rose above. St Joseph (1978, 284) has pointed out that this may indicate that the lower slopes of *Mons Graupius* were concave, which would have produced the spectacle referred to, whereas a convex slope would have tended to mask the higher ranks from the sight of those below (and made overall control of the Caledonian forces more difficult). The location of the native chariotry has given rise to some debate; the most natural interpretation of the phrase *media campi* would be 'the intervening level ground' (as Ogilvie and Richmond 1967, 272), but the suggestion has also been made (Burn 1953a, 15–2) that the Caledonian position straddled a pass or col with the infantry massed on the heights and the chariots occupying the low ground in the centre. It is difficult to believe, however, that so restrictive a position would have been assigned to what was essentially a highly mobile arm, designed for hit-and-run tactics rather than a massed charge and certainly not for defence (cf. Caesar,*B.G.* iv, 33).

The chariot crews consisted of drivers (normally the owners, and of a superior rank) and *propugnatores* who undertook the actual fighting. Their use as a preliminary 'softening-up' exercise, with the object of unsettling or even breaking up the ranks of the Roman front-line, would clearly involve their deployment in 'the intervening plain'. One can imagine them galloping at breakneck speed towards the Roman lines, wheeling at the last moment, and then with the slightest of checks to allow the spearmen to launch their missiles, scampering back across the plain. With less disciplined opponents

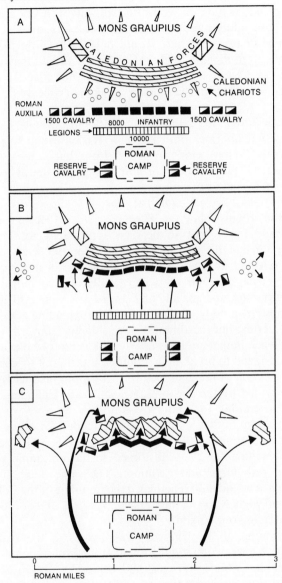

Figure 12. Idealised reconstruction of the successive phases of the battle, as described by Tacitus.

such tactics might have proved effective, but to a battle-hardened auxiliary these lightly-built two-wheeled speedsters, drawn by mettlesome ponies of no great size, would have given little trouble (cf. Powell 1963; 166; Piggott 1983, 217, 229–37); and all they achieved, as Tacitus says, was to fill the plain with noise and bustle; the determined attentions of the Roman cavalry soon cleared them from the field.

Agricola's order to extend the battle-line would have been executed with deliberate unhurried calm. It is uncertain how long this manoeuvre would have made Agricola's front, but on the assumption (Burn 1953a, 152) that *diductis ordinibus* implies a density of one file of four infantry men or two mounted troopers to each metre of front, the front would have extended at least 3.5 kilometres. By comparison, the English line at Hastings, where Harold deployed approximately 7,000 foot soldiers, was probably not more than 1 kilometre in length; and at Agincourt, for the final encounter, Henry V selected an even narrower front for an army of similar numerical strength (but of widely differing composition). At Bannockburn, the first assault of Edward II's vanguard may have been opposed by a body of some 3,500 foot extending across a front of 1.8 kilometres, but the thinness of this deployment was mitigated by the presence immediately to its front of a series of pits and other obstacles designed to break up a mounted attack, not to mention the natural protection of the Bannock Burn. A more instructive parallel may be provided by the Jacobite dispositions at Culloden, where a front-line accounting for about two-thirds of an army some 5,000 strong, drawn up in files six men deep, extended for more than 900 metres across Drummossie Moor (Prebble 1965, 74); these were mainly Highland infantry, accustomed to having ample room for manoeuvre with targe and claymore. The same need for sword-handling space would have lengthened the front-line of the Caledonian army beyond what Agricola might have expected, and hence aroused his fears of being outflanked.

The stationing of the legionary vexillations at the rear of the position was a not uncommon deployment for Roman commanders – Cerealis, under whom Agricola had served in Britain a decade earlier, had used similar tactics in AD 70 when facing the Batavian rebels at Vetera on the Rhine. It would be reasonable to assume that the legions occupied higher ground than the auxiliaries, since Agricola, who took up a position just in front of them, would have needed a suitable viewpoint from which to overlook and control the operations of the *auxilia*; moreover, if the *vallum* in front of which the legions were drawn up was the rampart of the army's overnight bivouac (and on the analogy of Caesar, *Bell. Civ.* iii, 95, 1, this seems the most probable interpretation), we would also expect the camp to be situated on ground that commanded the immediate vicinity. In the absence of precise information about the strength of Agricola's army, we can only speculate about the size of the marching camp. Assuming that at least 20,000 men were involved (see p. 43), one might imagine that the area of the camp could well have exceeded 25 hectares, but the fact that they were travelling light (*expedito exercitu*) may mean that the normal *pedaturae* (allotments of camping-space) were not in operation.

(iii/iv) *The Exchange of Missiles and Close-quarter Engagement*

As the maximum effective killing-range of a hand-thrown missile is about 30 metres, we may imagine that the action commenced with a general advance by the auxiliaries upon the enemy position. Normal tactics would have been for the troops to have followed up the launching of their spears with a charge, care being taken that no impulsion was lost between the falling of the volley of spears and the succeeding assault with the sword. In this case, however, it seems that the ability of the Caledonian front-rank warriors to avoid being struck by the Roman salvo, together with the persistent rain of missiles hurled by the ranks behind them (who had the additional advantage of height) checked the auxiliaries' closing charge. Consequently, Agricola had to renew the order to come to grips, and it probably required all the disciplined pertinacity of the 3,000 Batavian and Tungrian infantry to brave the withering enemy fire and bring their shorter stabbing blades to work inside the guard of the Caledonian front-line. The situation that then developed resembled in some ways that which won the close-quarter phase of the battle at Culloden, where a body of disciplined troops facing sword-wielding warriors directed their bayonets beneath the upraised sword-arm of the enemy assailing their right-hand neighbour, confident that they in turn would be protected from similar assault by the men that stood at

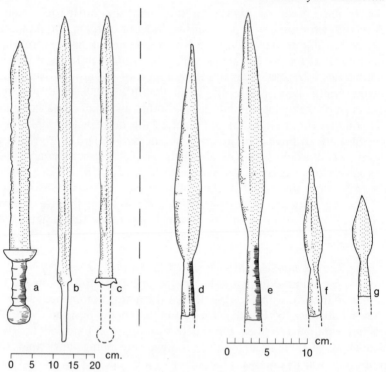

Figure 13. A selection of the kind of weapons used by Roman troops at Mons Graupius: a, *gladius*, or short sword; b, c, *spatha*, as used by auxiliary infantry and cavalry; d, e, lance-heads suitable for use by cavalry; f, g, spearheads.

their left shoulder. At Mons Graupius this concerted use of arms was supplemented by the possession of a shield with an iron boss that could be thrust in the enemy's face, knocking him off balance, as well as protecting the bearer. In the mean time the shorter blades of the auxiliary swords, 50–80 centimetres in length, with point as well as cutting edge (figure 13; Breeze *et al.* 1976, 83–4), did dreadful damage as they were jabbed at the unprotected face and neck, for it is unlikely that the average Caledonian warrior had previously encountered this lunging technique, against which his frail targe was totally inadequate and his own lack of body-armour made him hideously vulnerable. Sixty years later, it would appear, the same minuscule shields and absence of other defensive equipment again placed the native warrior at a grave disadvantage against the determined battalions of Rome (cf. Ritchie 1969, 31–40; see figure 14).

Figure 14. Roman cavalry troopers and defeated North Britons half a century after the battle at Mons Graupius, as depicted on Antonine Wall Distance Slabs: left, Summerston Farm slab; right, Bridgeness slab. In both scenes the tribesmen are stripped for action; it is unlikely that their weapons are accurate representations.

At this point in the battle the Batavians and Tungrians pressed home their attack and the Roman centre bulged forward with their advance uphill into the heart of the Caledonian army (a vivid picture in the Tacitean account, which surely stems from an eye-witness of the battle). To get further up the slopes of Mons Graupius the auxiliaries had to clamber over the bodies of the fallen, who were left on the bloodstained ground behind them (figure 15). Possibly there was an element of panic in the British ranks as the ferocity of the first clash broke upon them, and many of the fallen would have been knocked down without receiving a wound. This is the moment at

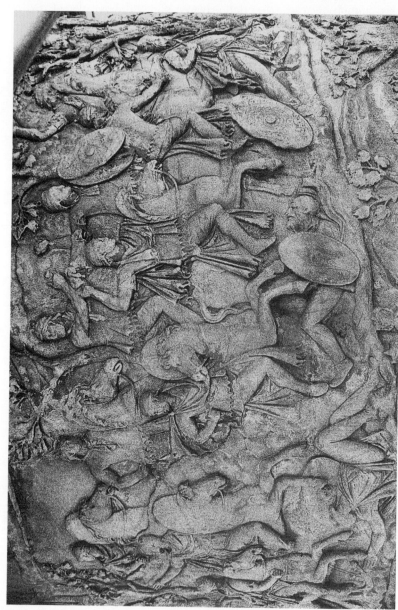

Figure 15. Roman auxiliary cavalry in action, a scene from Trajan's column.

which, paradoxically, the unity of the Roman line may have begun to dissolve, for if the onslaught was as efficient as Tacitus implies, the sheer bulk of prostrate bodies would have been enough to make it impossible to maintain regular dressing; similar problems are recounted in the descriptions of famous encounters of old (cf. Keegan 1978, 97–101). As the gaps opened in the front of battle, cavalry elements, probably those returning from the pursuit of the skirmishing charioteers, hastened to involve themselves in the conflict, side by side with their infantry comrades. Although their arrival lent fresh impetus to the assault and effectively mopped up any fighting that had spilled out behind the advancing cohorts, the troopers and their mounts were soon pinned in the melee, unable to assist materially and threatening to destabilise the position even further, a danger which was increased by stray horses and chariots roaming uncontrolled about the battlefield. Scholars rightly note that Tacitus' comment at this point *minimeque equestris ea pugnae facies erat* ('by no means like a cavalry engagement') is a literary cliché, borrowed from accounts of battles stretching back over the centuries to Cannae and the campaigns of Alexander the Great (cf. Ogilvie and Richmond 1967, 276–6; Burn 1953a, 154). There is no reason, however, to doubt that the point was worth making, since it heralded the approach of a turning-point in the fortunes of either side.

(v) *The Caledonian Outflanking Movement*

It seems probable that Calgacus was the first to see this as a critical moment in the battle. The bulk of the Roman auxiliary infantry had now been committed and probably much of the mounted strength was also inextricably embroiled in a struggle where the uphill toil and the shambles of war had slowed movement. Whatever the reason, he now chose to commit his own reserves, seeking to bring them round the side of the hill on either flank and launch an enveloping attack on the rear of the closely-packed *auxilia*. Alternatively, the Caledonian forces that now descended on the milling combatants may have been not so much reserves as lesser folk with inferior equipment and of little repute, who had not originally won a place in the battle array. The presence of these 'irregulars' on the higher ground behind the host of picked troops may have helped to swell the apparent strength of the Caledonian army in Roman eyes. The quoted figure of 30,000, which equals eighteenth-century government estimates of the maximum armed strength of all the Highland clans, seems an excessively high figure for the tribal levies of north-east Scotland in the Iron Age, unless these included followers as well as fully accoutred fighting men – not that the former element could be accounted of little worth in battle. It was the 'small folk' at Bannockburn whose arrival on the field of battle proved the last straw for Edward's army, even though the impact they made was mainly psychological.

(vi) *Roman Cavalry Riposte*

In the event it proved to be the ruin of the Caledonian army, for Agricola had wisely kept a mobile reserve of cavalry, possibly stationing them out of sight of the enemy (cf. Frontinus *Strategemata*, II, iii, 14). These he now launched from either wing, to fall on the charging enemy. The shock of their meeting may in some small way be recaptured, if one examines the relief sculpture of numerous tombstones erected in memory of Roman auxiliary troopers (figure 14) or the monumental celebrations of Roman victories (figure 15) and imagines the effect of a massed attack by a force two thousand strong, well mounted and efficiently led, upon a body of native troops with inferior weapons and in loose array. Probably the first assault with the lance would have sufficed to break up the charge, and thereafter a ranging pursuit of disheartened fugitives would have devolved into an exercise that was no more difficult, and probably a lot less hazardous, than pig-sticking; fleeing infantry are exceptionally vulnerable to such a form of warfare, as those who broke and ran before lancers in the Crimea and at Waterloo could testify. The small groups who stood and fought at close quarters would have found that the cavalrymen were equally dexterous with the swords that hung from their left shoulder. And it was probably with the latter weapons unsheathed that, on Agricola's orders, they turned from the chase and fell upon the flanks and rear of the main body of Caledonians, in many cases launching themselves with all the *élan* of a downhill gallop into the hapless native rear rankers. It may have been at this stage of the battle that Aulus Atticus was lost, for it is unlikely that at any previous time, when the fighting was uphill, he could have been carried into the enemy's midst, even on a spirited horse.

(vii) *The Enemy Routed*

Under the weight of this additional blow, particularly since it occasioned the violent physical disruption of the lines, the Caledonian army lost much of its cohesion, and began to scatter. At first, the native warriors appear to have withdrawn in groups (*agminibus*), which probably means that different clans rallied to their chieftains or kinsfolk; later, even the ties of loyalty and blood were insufficient to hold them together. We now hear a little more from Tacitus about the nature of the countryside nearby, for there were obviously woods or thickets deep enough to serve as suitable sites for ambushing those of the Roman auxiliaries who had flung caution to the winds in their pursuit. Yet even this attempt to snatch some kind of victory or honour from defeat proved fruitless, thanks to Agricola's vigilance. His rapid re-organisation of the units hunting down the fleeing enemy is naturally elaborated by his biographer, but in reality it was nothing more than a prudent commander might have done, and usually did, in many other ancient conflicts of which reports have come down to us: the Normans pursuing the English after Hastings were similarly near to chastisement but escaped it, allegedly because of Duke William's presence. Indeed, if we look beneath the bare words of Tacitus, it is possible to see the retrieval of near disaster, assuming that the phrase *acceptum aliquod vulnus* (would have sustained some casualties) is an understatement.

The number of Roman, or rather auxiliary, troops slain was remarkably small, for the figure of 360 given by Tacitus must be accepted as the officially recognised total, which could have been verified against extant archives in Rome at the time of writing. We may compare this with 50 dead and 259 wounded on the victorious side at Culloden, losses of only 3.5 per cent, against conservative estimates of 1,200 dead out of 5,000 odd in the Jacobite army, or almost 24 per cent. The comparison is instructive to the extent that a similar disparity existed in equipment and discipline between the two armies involved. Agincourt with a different kind of disparity produced similarly disproportional casualties, the French losing possibly 6,000 of the 25,000 that may have been committed. The Caledonian losses amounting to 10,000 which Tacitus reports need not therefore be totally rejected, although they are almost certainly inflated. Tacitus, to be fair, does not glory in the fact, nor does he baulk at stating in plain terms precisely what is meant: *passim arma et corpora et laceri artus et cruenta humus* – the reduplicated conjunction piles the pity of it in bulk no less than the actual heaps of slain. We must remember, however, that small though the Roman losses were reported to be, there would also have been wounded, at least three times as numerous as the dead. The picture of Agricola's subsequent triumphal progress to winter quarters must therefore be modified by the thought that he bore with him the equivalent of two cohorts of disabled troops. We may imagine what many of these wounds will have been, for despite their mail corselets and robustly made helmets (cf. Robinson, 1975, 45–106) the auxiliary infantry man or trooper who received the full force of a blow from one of the heavy Caledonian swords would have sustained serious injuries – deep cuts, amputated limbs, depressed fractures of the skull, and shattered bones. Still, they had at least a medical service on the spot to give them such comfort as ancient medicine could provide (Davies 1970). For the enemy no such provisions existed, and the character of their wounds was probably also more serious. Wounds to the head and face will have been common, few Caledonians having any form of protective helmet, and many would have been disabled by a wound in the abdomen and thorax, condemning them to a painful death through peritonitis or punctured lungs, if not loss of blood and shock. In other words, the prognosis for any but the lightly wounded among the native host would have been extremely poor. On the other hand, the fact that large numbers of Caledonians fought naked may have saved them, when wounded, from eventual septicaemia through the lodging of soiled clothing in the body cavities.

The practical question of what happened to the bodies of the dead remains to be considered, although without much hope of producing an informative answer. The Roman dead would doubtless have been accorded a military funeral in a mass grave, but whether by inhumation or cremation cannot be determined. Although there is contemporary evidence of inhumation practised by the Roman garrison at Camelon (Breeze *et al.* 1976), in the Roman Empire generally cremation appears to have become by that time the almost universal practice, and with a large number of corpses to dispose of, it may have been the preferred rite. In view of the exceptional problems on the Caledonian side, with a death-roll amounting to many thousands, it is perhaps pointless to examine the scattered instances of Iron Age burial, whether of warriors or unidentified persons, in Northern Britain. Burials in cists, even multiple burials in stone-lined graves have been reported (Longworth *et al.* 1966), but, if we assume that most of the dead would not have been left to moulder on the stricken field, then some form of communal tomb – massive pits, or gigantic cairns or barrows – would have had to be constructed; since the battle had been fought on home territory the first alternative is extremely unlikely – the piles of bones reported by Orderic Vitalis to be cumbering the ground at Stamford Bridge years after the fateful battle of 1066 were presumably those of the invading army and not native English. Even after the removal of the wounded and the slain, however, there would still have been a vast quantity of military equipment scattered across the field, and it is possible, as Dr Keppie recently pointed out (1980, 85) that the discovery of such wreckage may eventually indicate the actual field of battle, in the same way that vast assemblages of armour and weapons found at Alesia vividly illustrate the results of Caesar's victory over Vercingetorix in 52 BC (Harmand 1967), or the rusty harvest of munitions of war from the light friable soils in the valley of the Somme remind us of the suicidally brave offensive by the British regiments in 1916.

The morning after the battle found the Roman troops jubilant. Of the enemy there was nothing to be seen, and the brooding desolation of the field was accentuated by the silence of the surrounding hills and the smoke pall hanging over the deserted open settlements. The Caledonian army had not regrouped, but, in any case, the time for campaigning was past; the phrase *exacta aestate* ('summer being spent') means that it was now the second half of August, if not even later; Birley (1981, 77–8) argues that it was after the autumnal equinox (September 22–3), but if Tacitus took the equinox to represent the *flexus* ('turn') of autumn rather than the beginning (*Histories*, V, 32; Ogilvie and Richmond, 318), a somewhat earlier date must be presumed. Agricola therefore contented himself with a march down to the coast (*deducit*) to make contact with his fleet, which was presumably riding at anchor in some protected harbour – the autumn was not a time to be caught on the open sea. To reach the sea he had to cross the territory of the Boresti, a tribe whose location is completely unknown, despite the ingenuity of generations of scholars and amateur philologists, and who may have lain beyond or behind the field of battle, but probably not further distant than a day's march.

Agricola now gave orders for his fleet to make the circumnavigation of Britain, partly to overawe the tribes living beyond the area of campaigning – thus revealing that *Mons Graupius* did not in truth lie at the *terminus Britanniae*, as had been claimed – partly to complete a chapter of exploration. How long the voyage took we cannot be sure, but Tacitus has already told us (*Agricola*, x, 4) that by the time the fleet hove in sight of *Thule* (the Orkneys or Shetlands), winter was drawing near, i.e. that it was late October. This would seem to indicate that the later of the two dates for the battle should in fact be favoured, but we do not know the circumstances of the voyage between the meeting with Agricola and the arrival off the Orkneys; contrary winds and currents (*mare pigrum et grave remigantibus*) or clashes with northern tribes while putting in for water or reconnaissance may have presented problems similar to those encountered the summer before by the Usipi. At length the fleet found a following wind, and came to berth without loss at the harbour named *Portus Trucculensis*, which many assume to be the base from which it was then operating. The precise location of the harbour and the meaning of the opaque phraseology used by Tacitus to describe this phase of the operations has engendered much scholarly comment, especially in recent times (cf. Burn 1969, 59; Ogilvie and Richmond 1967, 282–3; Reed 1971, 147–8; Hind 1974). Although attempts have been made to show that the *Portus* was an anchorage on the north-west coast of Scotland, possibly the farthest point reached in naval reconnaissance two years earlier, the sense of the passage demands that a complete circumnavigation should have been made in the final year of Agricola's governorship thus setting the seal on his achievements. The circumnavigation, however, need not have been inconsistent with stopping temporarily at a point already reached by a different route. The identification of such a stopover in fact may be suggested by the variant form of the place-name, *Trutulensis*. Although suitable explanations and etymology have been offered for the other (Rivet and Smith, 1979, s.v.), it is more conceivable that similarity to the adjective *truculentus* procured its acceptance in the manuscripts. Without descending into minutely detailed argument – (inclusion of a variant reading later mis-read: *thu/tulensem* becoming *tru/tulensem*) – suffice it to say that the original might perhaps have been *Portus Thulensis*, i.e. the harbour at Thule (the Orkneys or Shetlands), within sight of which Agricola's fleet certainly operated at some time in his governorship (*Agricola*, x, 4). The importance of this exploit to the study of *Mons Graupius* lies in the point made by Birley (1981, 78) that Agricola's final dispatch to Domitian included news of the fleet's exploits and safe return to base – an accomplishment that probably could not have been reported before November at the earliest. It is thus entirely possible that Domitian's allegedly farcical triumph after the conclusion of the Chattan campaign in 83 preceded by a little space the news of Agricola's real successes in Britain, a relationship which would allow us to date his governorship to 77–83 rather than 78–84 (see below, pp. 114–15).

At all events, a battle had been won, and at astoundingly little cost, but the remarkable thing about it may have been, as Webster has observed (1969, 229–30), not that it resulted in victory, but that the Caledonians allowed it to take place. The results of their strategic blunder will be considered in the final chapter; first we must consider where it befell.

FOUR

Locating the Battlefield:
Antiquarian Essays

DEEPER consideration of the nature and impact of Agricola's victory at *Mons Graupius* can be justified by the refinement it adds to our appreciation of the Roman period in Scotland, but the sceptic may ask why we should concern ourselves about the precise location. Apart from the basic advantage of knowing how far Roman military plans were advanced by the Flavian conquest of the North, there remains the simple pretext of human curiosity. The enthusiasm of the early antiquaries on this issue was also fuelled by a respect for the soldierly virtues and *amor patriae*. The eccentric Earl of Buchan, who founded the Society of Antiquaries of Scotland in 1781, gave rhapsodic utterance to such views: 'I studied the language and manners of the Gael, examined the remains of their rude antiquities and with the speech of Galcacus in my hand adored the Spirit of my Ancestors on the footsteps of their Glory' (Glasgow University Library, Murray MS 502/61). No lesser zeal animated the breast of Scott's whimsical Antiquary, Jonathan Oldbuck, author of that oft-quoted treatise *Essay upon Castrametation, with some Particular Remarks upon the Vestiges of Ancient Fortifications lately discovered by the Author at the Kaim of Kinprunes*; Scott would have been delighted to learn that his fictional Kaim, reputedly the scene of Calgacus' defeat, had so established itself in the country's tradition-ary history that not fifteen years ago an officer of the National Monuments Archive was requested to supply its precise map-reference for inclusion in a local archaeological register!

This happy blend of fact and imagination finds an early parallel in the first recorded attempt to present Tacitus' story of the Caledonian campaigns of Agricola to a Scottish audience. *The Chronicles of Scotland*, compiled at some time before 1527 by Hector Boece, first Principal of King's College, Aberdeen, drew equally upon history

Figure 16. Detail of frontispiece map in Roy's *Military Antiquities of the Romans in North Britain* (1793), showing traditional location of the battle at Mormond Hill, Grampian Region.

and imagination, as the following excerpts, presented in the Scots translation of 1531 by John Bellenden, amply demonstrate:

> Sik things done be Agricola, ane convencioun wes maid in Atholl of all pepill under Galdus' empire, abiding the King of Pichtis and his army to resist the Romanis. The Pichtis war

cumand than oure the montanis of Granzeben, quhilk rynnis fra
the fute of Dee to Dounbritan . . . (IV, xii)

We are in a curious unhistorical world, where Picts, Danes, and Scots
under the leadership of Galdus (Calgacus) prepare to unite in
opposition to a Roman invader. The mountains of Granzeben (which
Camden, through Holinshed, transformed to Gransbain) are none
other than *Mons Graupius*, their location between Aberdeen and
Dumbarton identifying them as the entire Grampian massif! The
ensuing clash between the Romans and the northern confederacy,
assigned by Bellenden to the seventh year of Agricola's governorship, would appear to be the equivalent of the night assault on the
Ninth Legion which actually occurred during his sixth campaign
(Boece IV, xiv). An extra summer of warfare is then interpolated, in
which we learn the tribes defended themselves against the Roman
advance:

moir be skarmusing than ony plane bataill . . . But the Romanis,
ilk day moir insolent be frequent victoriis, traistit nathing
unvincibill to thame, and past throw the Callendair Wode with
purpos to serch all the last boundis of Albion, and becaus thai
war stoppit be the strait ground thereof, thai come oure the
watter of Awmound and sett down thair campe nocht far fra
Dunkeld, quhair Tay rynnis nicht profounde . . . The Pychtis,
effrayit be the cuming of the Romanis sa fer within thair landis,
brynt ane riche town callit Inchetuthill (*Tulina*), quhilk stude
apoun the river of Taya, that the samyn suld be na refuge to thair
inimeis, and fled with thair wyffis, children, and guids to the
Montanis of Granzeben.

Winter then put an end to hostilities, and in the following summer
Agricola is supposed to have ordered his fleet to circumnavigate
Britain; however, having foolishly entrusted the guiding of the
expedition to a number of native pilots, the *praefectus classis* was
soon mortified to find his ships in all manner of difficulties, until
eventually:

ther navy wes drevin to craggis and sand beddis be force of
streme and contrarious fludes. Agricola, na thing knawing of the
calamite falling to his navy, buildit ane brig of tre oure Tay with
mair expedicioun than ingyne of man mycht traist, and trans-
portit his army be the samyn nocht far fra the fute of Granzeben,

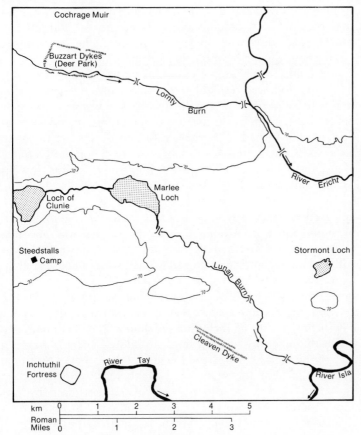

Figure 17. The setting for the 'Stormont' scenario; only the fortress at Inchtuthil and the labour-camp at Steedstalls are Roman monuments, the others being medieval or prehistoric.

levand behind him mony strang weer men to keep the said brig unbett down be gyle or violence of inimeis. The Pychtis, nocht effrayit of his cuming, send thair ambassadouris to Galdus to shaw him the appering danger to bath thair realmez and desyrit him to cum with all his powere to revenge the iniuris done be the

Romanis. Bot Galdus gaderit afoir thair cuming xl^m chosin and rank men out of all boundis under his empire . . . and sone eftir brocht his army with huge labour oure the montanis of Granzeben, quhair he mett the remanent army of Pichtis and Danys quhilkis wer assemblyt in that samyn maner. (IV, xiv)

The battle that followed resulted in the victory of the Roman legions – even Boece could not overturn the decisions of history – but, in his account (IV, xv), it was by the narrowest of margins, the tide of battle being eventually turned in Agricola's favour by the arrival of the 'Almanis', possibly a reference to the auxiliary cohorts of Germans, Batavians, and Tungrians mentioned or implied by Tacitus. It would appear that this melancholy event was attended by portents which Tacitus did not think fit to describe to his readers:

> ane grete noumer of schippis wer sene in the air. Mony schouris of stanis ranyt in Athoill, siclyke in Anguse was ane huge schower of paddokkis. Ane monstour was sene in Inchtuthill with double membris of man and woman with sa abhominabill a figure that it was distroyit be the pepill. (IV, xvi)

Although Boece was not explicit in specifying the site of the battle of *Mons Graupius*, his implication that it was north of the Tay and possibly in the vicinity of Inchtuthil led James Playfair, minister of the parish of Bendothy in Perthshire, to adduce the *Chronicles* as evidence of the battle having been fought in the district of Stormont, between the loch of that name and Dunkeld. Playfair's account (1797), based on local tradition, was further bolstered by false etymology – a frequent resort of the early antiquary – Stormont being explained as the 'Stour' (struggle) -ment', or main battle. Needless to say, the neighbourhood was ransacked to provide suitable 'scenery' for the occasion (figure 17). The Buzzart Dykes, a medieval deer-dyke to the north-west of Blairgowrie, was hailed as the camp of Calgacus before the battle, and the Garrydrums ridge upon which it lies identified as *Graupius* itself. The Romans were said to have had two fortified bases in the area, one at Inchtuthil and the other at Meikleour; the latter was defended on two sides by the Rivers Tay and Isla, and elsewhere by the Cleaven Dyke which was assumed to be the *vallum* in front of which Agricola stationed his legions as the final reserve. The Cleaven Dyke still survives as a broad low bank, flanked on either side by flat-bottomed ditches, and its course may still be traced for some 2.7 kilometres through forestry plantations to the north east of the village of Meikleour, but it is certainly not the fortified perimeter of a camp, and although identified as a Roman boundary-mark by Richmond (1940, 40), it may possibly be many centuries older. The curious 'quarry-holes' known as Steed Stalls which are situated within the Roman temporary camp upon the Hill of Gourdie to the north of Inchtuthil were also written into the scenario, their purpose being to hold the hundred horses of a detachment keeping watch on the northern approaches to the Tay. What clinched the matter for Playfair, as it did for so many others on the same quest, was that the locality abounded in cairns; the course of the battle could thus be followed by a series of funereal fingerposts that extends across three parishes!

Playfair's conjectures represent the dying bars, but not absolutely the last notes, of 'an auld sang' that had appealed to generations of Scots enchanted by the ancient glories of their kingdom. The need for a more critical approach to the problem, particularly in the use of surviving remains and the literary sources, as well as the relationship of both to Scottish topography, was beginning to be appreciated. It was hoped, in the words of one of Playfair's contemporaries and rivals in the hunt, that the time was

> at last come, when, under the influence of the Antiquarian Society established in Scotland, our antiquaries will be rescued from the mists of ignorance, and the phantoms of credulity, – when the fabrications of monks will be treated with contempt, and the prejudices of national vanity no longer will warp the judgement, but truth and sound criticism succeed in room of both. (Grant, 1822, 32)

Before such pious hopes were fulfilled, an ocean of academic ink required to be spilt recording the foibles and lesser lunacies of successive generations of antiquarian sleuths as they tracked Agricola through the brakes and brambles of Tacitean prose. Colonel Shand, for example, was in favour of Fendoch, at the mouth of the Sma' Glen, where tradition (e.g *O.S.A*, xv, 256–7) recorded the existence of a Roman camp long before the Flavian fort was proved by excavation, the adjacent native stronghold of Dunmore representing the ground occupied by the Caledonians; Horsley (1732, 44) feeling, as did Shand, that the battle must have taken place in close proximity

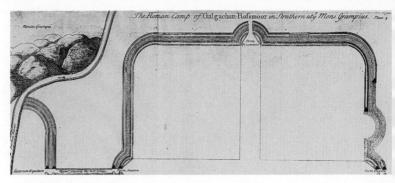

Figure 18. Detail of plan of Dalginross fort and camp in Gordon's *Itinerarium Septentrionale* (1727).

to the Grampian massif, expressed an interest in Fortingall in Glen Lyon, to the north of Loch Tay; but, despite the scenic attractions and wealth of tradition associated with the spot, the rectilinear earthwork situated there is of medieval origin and its nearest link with Rome is in its proximity to the venerable churchyard-yew, which folk-myth associates with Pontius Pilate and which aerial reconnaissance indicates may be at the centre of an Early Christian monastic settlement.

In the early days of fieldwork, antiquaries were greatly struck by the impressive earthwork remains at Ardoch and Dalginross. Most were persuaded by the Tacitean account that the events of the sixth season had taken place in Fife, the location of the night-attack on the Ninth Legion being Lochore at the foot of the southern slopes of Benarty Hill; unfortunately, no trace survives of the rectangular enclosure which once occupied the site, but it seems more likely to have been of prehistoric or medieval origin than Roman. After wintering in Fife – as some had it, on the summit of Dunearn Hill above Burntisland – Agricola was believed to have marched north-westwards through Glendevon and Gleneagles towards the mountains that beckoned from the north side of upper Strathearn. At Ardoch the Roman army bivouacked for the night and prepared itself for battle. The scene of the actual conflict was disputed. Sibbald (1707, 37; 1711, 101) presumed that it took place between Ardoch and the Ochil Hills, but Chalmers (1807; i, 112–13) and Stuart (1845, 70–8) argued strongly for Ardoch moor, to the north of the complex of Roman fortifications, where the existence of a large ditch, first recognised by Gordon (1726, 42), was taken to indicate the position occupied by Agricola's legions *pro vallo*. More significance was found, however, in the fact that eastern outliers of the Beinn Odhar massif ascended from the north-west margin of the proposed battlefield, and it was doubtless these that the Caledonian levies were thought to have occupied.

The site had already been examined and dismissed by Alexander Gordon (1726, 36–41), on the grounds that the Caledonian position could not be said to be part of the Grampian range, while the size of the fort at Ardoch precluded it from accommodating more than a small part of the army of Agricola; for some reason, Gordon disregarded the remains of temporary camps lying immediately outside the fort, possibly because his attention had been caught by the complex at Dalginross, on the south-western outskirts of Comrie (figure 18). Although he was correct in thinking that the camp, with its distinctive Stracathro-type gates (see above p. 32), was of Flavian date, its area, 9.5 hectares, was certainly not sufficient to accommodate the Agricolan force at *Mons Graupius*. Gordon got round this problem by assuming that the camp was assigned solely to the 8000 auxiliary infantry, with the cavalry lodged in either the adjacent fort or its associated enclosure, communication between the two being provided by a raised *agger*; he did not explain where the legionary element encamped meanwhile. From the plan of the site with which he illustrated his proposals, it will be clear that Gordon did not trouble himself with the niceties of archaeological surveying, but relied instead on fieldworker's instinct – an intuitive guide which, when wedded to experience and discrimination, probably counts for more than logical deduction in the search for lost fragments of antiquity. In Gordon's case, however, the discriminative element appears to have succumbed to an excess of enthusiasm, and in the end we find him buttressing his argument with the most far-fetched etymological propositions, namely that the site was known locally as 'Galgachan Rossmoor', an imposture which failed to convince even antiquaries hailing from south of Cheviot (Horsley 1734, 44). Much may nevertheless be forgiven to one who flung himself into the

Figure 19. Roy's plan of Dalginross, where it was believed the Ninth Legion had been attacked in Agricola's penultimate campaign.

pursuit of antiquity with such whole-hearted zeal; the following passage conveys the essence of his approach:

> Moreover, the Situation of this Ground is so very exact with the Description given by Tacitus, that in all my Travels through *Britain*, I never beheld any Thing with more Pleasure, it being directly at the Foot of the *Grampian Hills*; besides there are the *Colles*, or small rising Grounds, on which the *Caledonians* were placed before the Battle, and also the high Hill on which the Body of the *Caledonian* Army lay, and from which they came down upon the *Roman*: Nor is it difficult on viewing this Ground, to guess at the Place where the *Covinnarii*, or Charioteers, stood. In fine, to an Antiquary, this is a ravishing Scene . . . (Gordon 1726, 40)

It was this ravishment of the senses, we may imagine, that Scott had in mind when delineating the character of Jonathan Oldbuck, particularly as a protagonist of the Kaim of Kinprunes; Grant, too, may have referred to it in his dismissive 'phantoms of credulity'. As well they might, seeing that the later half of the eighteenth century had shown what a wealth of additional reliable information could be produced by a more practical approach. In this new development the military profession made the most useful contribution, Colonel Shand, who has already been mentioned, and Generals Melville and Roy being pre-eminent, whether by reason of their discoveries of Roman marching-camps or their discussion of Roman campaiging in Scotland. It is plain that all these workers in the field were inspired by a disgust with the impractical theorising of 'unmilitary Antiquaries', as Melville put it (Stuart 1868, 30), and their success stemmed partly from the fact that, as serving officers in North Britain after the '45, they had acquired first-hand experience of the problems facing a Lowland army operating against a mainly Highland power-base. Of even greater significance was their participation in the Military Survey of the mainland of Scotland, the forerunner of the Ordnance Survey mapping agency which in modern times so delights and informs the lover of the British countryside. The study of terrain, which sprang from such political and professional requirements, was thus seen to be the only satisfactory basis for an examination of the Agricolan campaigns. William Roy, who devoted much of his masterpiece *Military Antiquities of the Romans in North Britain* to the consideration of this period, made specific reference to this line of research in his introductory remarks:

> The nature of a country will always, in a great degree, determine the principles upon which every war there must be conducted. In the course of many years, a morassy country may be drained; one that was originally covered with wood, may be laid open; or an open country may be afterwards inclosed; yet while the ranges of mountains, the long extended valleys, and remarkable rivers, continue the same, the reasons of war cannot essentially change. Hence it will appear evident, that what, with regard to situation, was an advantageous post when the Romans were carrying on their military operations in Britain, must, in all essential respects, continue to be a good one now; proper allowance being made for the difference of arms, and other changes which have taken place between the two periods.

The same criteria may still be usefully employed in modern archaeological survey, even when the surveyor enjoys an aerial viewpoint. The close comparability of Roy's military experience with that of a foot-soldier in Roman times – in respect of movement and manoeuvre – invests his opinions, and those of his contemporaries, with considerable value, and a quality that is lacking in appreciations by unmilitary scholars of a later, mechanised age. Basing his judgement upon a close study of Roman marching-camps in the field, as well as a critical perusal of the text of Tacitus, Roy declared (1793, 84) that it was 'beyond possibility of doubt, that the country to the eastward of the Tay was the scene of Agricola's operations during his seventh campaign'. Assuming that the camps of the 53-hectare series were those that had accommodated the Agricolan army, he toyed with the idea that the most northerly example then known, at Battledykes Oathlaw, roughly half-way between Kirriemuir and Brechin, might have been the last bivouac before the great battle. In that event, the Roman troops would have had to march at least four miles to reach even the fringes of the Grampian Hills, crossing the South Esk in their advance. Reluctantly, therefore, he resisted the attraction of the camp's apposite place-name, and concluded that the existence of a camp at Keithock to the north of Brechin, although only half as big as Oathlaw, was evidence of penetration even farther into Strathmore. Roy continued:

Figure 20. Detail of the map at the end of Roy's *Military Antiquities*, showing plan of Raedykes camp based on Barclay's original survey, as well as suggested site of battle on Kempstone Hill (top right).

Somewhere, therefore, about Fettercairn, Montboddo, or perhaps even still nearer to Stonehaven, it would seem probable that the battle may have happened; but unless a number of old Roman and Caledonian arms should, by mere accident, be dug up in the neighbourhood of those places, or that the vestiges of a camp should be discovered fronting one or other of them, sufficient to contain Agricola's whole army, we never can hope to ascertain the particular spot. Many thousand chances there must be to one against it ever being hit upon by either means; yet as so many camps have been found to exist in whole or in part, this, of the two methods, seems to be what would promise most success. The most likely places to examine and search for such vestiges, would therefore appear to be on the south side of the valley near Lawrence Kirk, Keir, or Drumliethy. That Agricola would choose this side seems probable, since the enemy being in possession of the Grampians, he would not have thought it consistent with providence to have encamped close under the hills which they occupied'. (1793, 86–7)

The worth of Roy's method is indicated by the fact that, in due course, a large temporary camp was in fact discovered at 'Keir' (now Kair House) during aerial reconnaissance by Professor St Joseph (1951, 65); the weakness lies in his uncritical use of structural evidence, it being impossible to be certain, as his immediate successors pointed out, that the camps in question were really built by Agricola's troops.

Although Roy put the final touches to the manuscript of *Military Antiquities* about 1777, it is evident (Macdonald 1916, 324–32) that he subsequently heard about the interest which had been aroused by the re-investigation of the site at Raedykes, some 5 kilometres to the north of Stonehaven, which had been first recorded as a Roman work by the antiquary Maitland (1757, i, 202). In fact, Maitland had been so convinced of its nature that he did not hesitate to claim it as the camp of Agricola before *Mons Graupius*, adding 'there is not the least room to doubt of this place's being the spot whereon the battle was fought'. Roy was clearly of the same opinion, for he prepared two drawings of the site from accurately surveyed material furnished to him, by some undisclosed means, after 1785, and entitled each of them 'Plan of Agricola's Camp called Rae Dykes'; those responsible for the posthumous publication of *Military Antiquities* not only saw to the incorporation of the Raedykes plan in the series of plates, but also included the site, duly labelled *Cast. Agricolae* in the map of Roman Scotland which appears as plate 1 of that volume (figure 16).

What Roy actually thought about the significance of the camp is not on record, but it is highly probable that he would have agreed with the group of scholars and antiquaries who recognised in it the evidence of Agricola's famous victory. Perhaps he would have opposed the structural interpretation which they offered; for example, Robert Barclay of Urie, the local landowner, (1777) identified it as the bivouac of Agricola's convoy *after* the engagement, the troops having set out from a now lost rectilinear fortification at Arduthy, immediately to the north of Stonehaven (A on figure 23), and closed with Calgacus on Kempstone Hill. The actual scene of the battle was indicated by a cairnfield and three burial cairns (as shown on figure 20) which Barclay took to be the resting-place of some of the Caledonian dead. This interpretation was adopted, almost word for word, by Lord Buchan (1786) and re-used by John Stuart of Inchbreck, Professor of Greek in the University of Aberdeen (1822), with the important alteration that Raedykes was thought to be too irregular on plan to be of Roman origin and had therefore to be identified as the camp which held the Caledonian army. Stuart also pointed to two other discoveries which in his eyes confirmed the association between this nexus of structures and the battle of *Mons Graupius* (1822, 301; cf. also Douglas 1782, 261); these included the finding of bronze spear heads 'in a moss hard by' and in the ditch of Raedykes 'a small hoop or ring of iron . . . which could be imagined useful for no other purpose than to contain the axle of one of the Caledonian war chariots'. Subsequently, a complete wheel was dug up inside the camp, and a third wheel-fragment was found by Sir George Macdonald, again in the ditch, during excavation (1916, 343). For Stuart, however, the clinching argument was the opening of 'a pretty large Tumulus or Barrow' in 1812 on or near the rectilinear enclosure at Arduthy, since it clearly indicated to him the spot on which the Romans had burned and laid their dead to rest. It was with some satisfaction, therefore, that he found himself able to claim:

> Here then, at length, has been the only particular wanting to determine the site of this battle. For here every circumstance concurs in pointing out this place as the real scene of the conflict between Agricola and Galgacus; a combination no where else to be found along the whole chain of the Grampian mountains . . .;

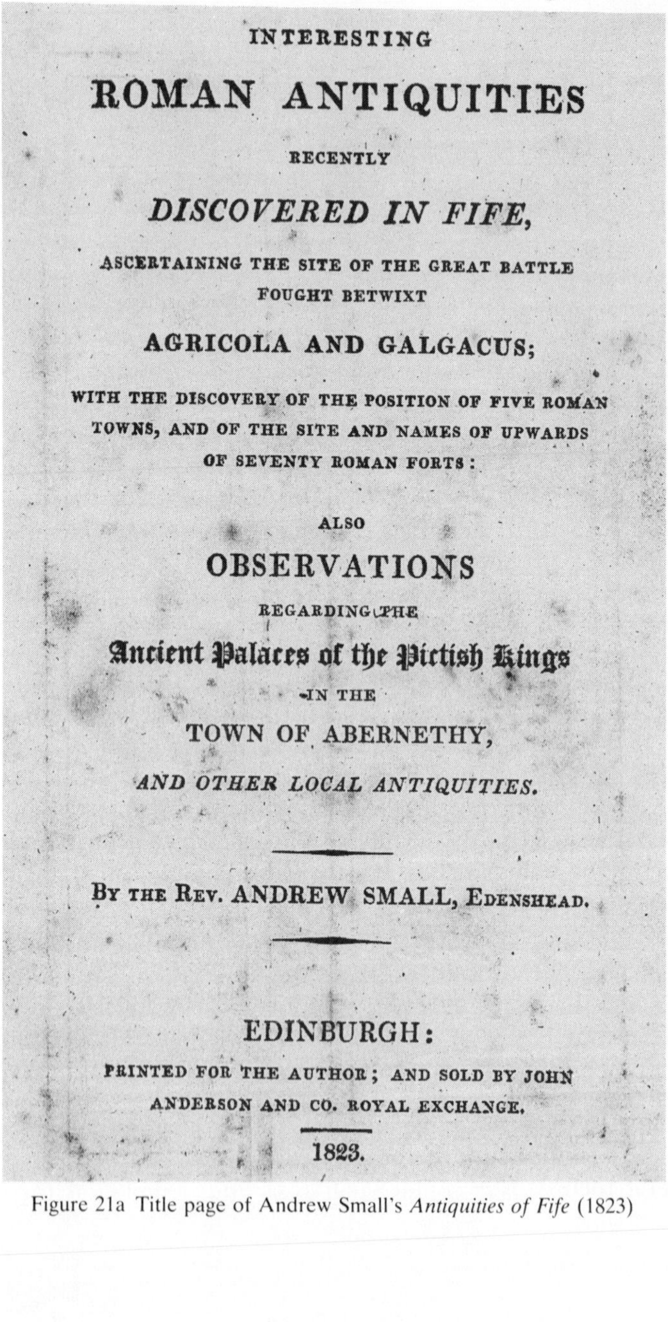

INTERESTING

ROMAN ANTIQUITIES

RECENTLY

DISCOVERED IN FIFE,

ASCERTAINING THE SITE OF THE GREAT BATTLE
FOUGHT BETWIXT

AGRICOLA AND GALGACUS;

WITH THE DISCOVERY OF THE POSITION OF FIVE ROMAN
TOWNS, AND OF THE SITE AND NAMES OF UPWARDS
OF SEVENTY ROMAN FORTS :

ALSO

OBSERVATIONS

REGARDING THE

Ancient Palaces of the Pictish Kings

IN THE

TOWN OF ABERNETHY,

AND OTHER LOCAL ANTIQUITIES.

———

By THE REV. ANDREW SMALL, EDENSHEAD.

———

EDINBURGH:

PRINTED FOR THE AUTHOR; AND SOLD BY JOHN
ANDERSON AND CO. ROYAL EXCHANGE.

———

1823.

Figure 21a Title page of Andrew Small's *Antiquities of Fife* (1823)

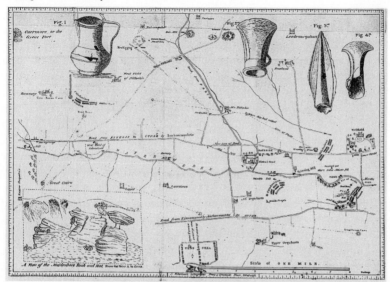

Figure 21b Battlefield of Meralsford below the Lomond Hills, Fife, as presented by Andrew Small.

and here, it is presumed, that this much disputed point will be invariably fixed, and universally acknowledged to be so. (Stuart 1822, 302)

It must have pained and surprised him to read, not a year later, an almost fabulous account of the battle, after the manner of the older antiquarians, set in the county of Fife, at the foot of the northern slopes of the Lomond Hills. For the Revd Andrew Small, the author of this work (1823), it was as if Roy and his immediate successors had never written. The character of the piece is amply revealed by the title-page (figure 21a), where, apart from the site of the battle, the discovery of no fewer than five Roman towns and 'upwards of seventy Roman forts' is confidently claimed. In the pages of Small's account we are once more in an uncritical and untutored world, where Iron Age forts, standing stones, cairns, cists and all manner of artefacts of the first and second millennia BC, not to mention late medieval objects, are pressed into service as witnesses to the veracity of the general theory. Nor could Small resist the temptation to read a

Roman origin or a fictitious significance into the place-names of the locality: Urquhart, applied to several farms to the south of Gateside (where the Roman army built one of its many camps; see figure 21b), is ingeniously derived from 'Orreaquarta'; Peat Hill is seen as a corruption of Peace-hill, the mound erected by the Romans in commemoration of a glorious victory; and Meralsford on the River Eden, is the 'Marvellous ford', where the streams of Eden ran miraculously encrimsoned with blood from the innumerable dead. It would be churlish, however, to leave this entertaining work of fiction, composed by Small with such laborious toil and in the teeth of severe physical disabilities – 'what by head-achs, and other complaints peculiar to a bilious habit' – without conceding that, at the very least, his labours served to put on record a considerable number of archaeological discoveries relating to earlier periods than the Roman, which might otherwise have gone largely unnoticed.

The same cannot, however, be said of the paper written by Lt.-Col. Miller and read to the Society of Antiquaries of Scotland over the winter of 1829/30. The preface to his account (1857, 19–20) would appear to indicate a line of enquiry similar to that followed by General Roy, in which the textual evidence was examined in the light of evidence presented by Roman structures and local topography; ominously, however, Miller allotted a role to tradition, which he considered to be 'oftentimes . . . correct as to leading facts, although it is seldom to be depended on when it descends into particulars'. Betrayed or seduced by this confidence, he followed the older antiquaries in presuming that Agricola had spent his sixth year of office campaigning in Fife, the Ninth Legion being assaulted near Lochore; at the end of this engagement the Caledonians fled in disorder through Portmoak Moss, scattering, as was their wont, bronze 'battle-axes' and arrow-heads of flint, while the Roman troops established their winter-quarters on the summit of Dunearn Hill, above Burntisland. In the next season Agricola marched north to Markinch, having learned that the Caledonian army had occupied a strong position on the Lomond Hills, and crossing the River Eden stationed his troops at Pitlour on one of the hills overlooking Strathmiglo, roughly 7 kilometres distant from the enemy (figure 22). Once there, he 'seems to have waited patiently until the advanced season of the year, and the want of provisions, compelled his

Figure 22. View of the Lomond Hills from the West; to the left lies the valley of the River Eden and the 'battlefield' of Meralsford.

opponents to quit their position'. The Caledonians were imagined to have descended the steep northern face of the Lomonds and crossed the River Eden at Merlsford – for Miller, too, was convinced that the old tradition of a battle at Merlsford could refer to none other than that between Calgacus and Agricola. In the meantime, the Romans had descended from their camp at Pitlour (which was, nevertheless, not left entirely unguarded, because in Miller's view 'an hospital may have been established there after the battle, for the wounded, as the nearest station'). After the bloody encounter at the ford, the battle seems to have rolled for 5 kilometres or so to the west, a second action developing when the Caledonian reserves attempted to cross to the north bank of the Eden to help their faltering comrades, only to be repulsed by the fresh regiments of cavalry whom Agricola then launched upon their flank. Agricola's movements after the victory are briefly described: the fugitive Caledonians were pursued through the Ochil Hills, and the Roman army, fording the Earn near Forteviot, made its way to the Tay at Perth, where direct contact was at last made with the fleet; previously, Miller implied, communication had been maintained by signalling from high ground north of Pitlour to where it lay at anchor in the Tay estuary; thereafter, Agricola is presumed to have set about constructing permanent garrison-posts to guard the overrun country, a reasonable assumption were it not that the list of sites then constructed comprises an indiscriminate medley of Roman, prehistoric, medieval and entirely imaginary structures!

If it has any value, other than that of curiosity, Miller's account furnishes an eloquent example of how strong a hold traditional history exerted on the mind of even the professionally skilled researcher, although it must be remembered that, like Andrew Small, Lt.-Col. Miller had close ties with the area in question, his family owning the lands of Urquhart to the south of Gateside. The reader may well ponder whether the two roughly contemporary nineteenth-century effusions about the site of *Mons Graupius* did not perhaps spring from some local rivalry; at any rate, neither contributed significantly to the quest, for more rigorous scholarship and a closer approach to the archaeological method were, in the hands of others, already beginning to make an impact. The way ahead was to be charted by the impartial historian and the archaeologist.

FIVE

Locating the Battlefield:
Archaeologists at Work

THE first three decades of the twentieth century saw sweeping advances in the development of archaeological skills, some with particular relevance to Roman Scotland. For most of the period, attention was concentrated on the study of permanent forts and, on the construction of a historical framework into which the results of excavation or fieldwork, and literary, epigraphic, and numismatic evidence, might be harmoñiously incorporated. Curle's work at Newstead (1911) and Macdonald's second magisterial volume on the Antonine Wall (1934) are splendid instances of the processes of critical analysis and synthesis that were then taking place. In the context of such striving for a well-founded basis to an infant discipline, it is not surprising that little time could be spared for the pursuit of a chimaera like the battlefield of *Mons Graupius*. Typical of such self-denial are Macdonald's treatment (1916) of the potentially emotive evidence at Raedykes (a 'Caledonian chariot-wheel') and the terse comments on *Mons Graupius* in the Furneaux and Anderson edition of the *Agricola* (1922). What triggered the renewal of interest in the search was the dawning of the age of aerial archaeology.

The old antiquarian tradition was not completely extinct, however. A curious work, whose subtitle – *A Saga of the Caledonian Race* (Pitblado, 1935) – conveys something of its character, purported to cast new light upon the problem of the Roman invasions of North Britain by claiming that in the 1st century AD the sea-level was approximately 30 metres higher than it is at present. Such arbitrary inundation, which extended the estuary of the Forth to a point only a few kilometres short of the eastern shore of Loch Lomond, and widened the Earn into an arm of the sea reaching almost as far as Strageath, would obviously have presented a Roman invader with

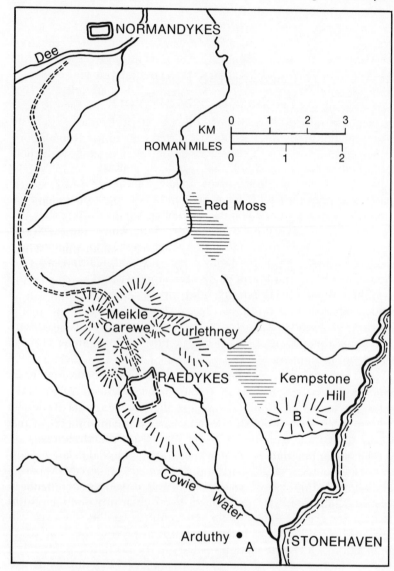

Figure 23. O. G. S. Crawford's choice for the battlefield – Raedykes: A, position of suspected Roman earthwork; B, traditional battle-site.

problems not previously considered by scholars. According to Pitblado (1935, 88–90), Agricola shipped his army from Camelon to the 'inlet' of Clackmannan, and then, marching 'round the head of the Devon fiord', advanced north-westwards through the Ochil Hills to meet the enemy on 'the arena of the now famous golf course of Gleneagles'! Scarcely less remarkable is Pitblado's attempt (97–106, 140–4) to show that the casualty figures provided by Tacitus were deliberately distorted to conceal the extent of Roman losses; by assuming that the total of 360 dead referred only to the Roman-born officers of auxiliary units, which were annihilated along with their commanders, he argued that the 'victory' at *Mons Graupius* cost Rome over 30,000 troops, or about 66 per cent of a field-force which was originally far superior in strength to that of the Caledonians.

The first archaeological air survey in Scotland appears to have been undertaken by O. G. S. Crawford, Archaeology Officer of the Ordnance Survey, in 1930, and about the same time Wing-Commander Insall of the Royal Air Force, while engaged in operational flying, took occasional photographs of interesting earth-works in Fife and Clydesdale. Crawford's second pioneering sortie (1939) displayed more amply the potential rewards of aerial reconnaissance in Scotland, and in 1944, after an interval occasioned by the War, the torch was caught up by Professor (then Dr) J. K. S. St Joseph, to be borne gloriously over a career that extended for some thirty-six years in the service of the Committee for Aerial Photography in the University of Cambridge (St Joseph 1976). This active reconnaissance was also supplemented by the results of routine inspection of vertical air photographs carried out by officers of the Royal Commission on the Ancient and Historical Monuments of Scotland over the same period (Maxwell 1978, 38), and in latter years by the Commission's independent programme of air survey (Maxwell 1983c, 27). In this chapter we will note some of the recent contenders for the site of the battle, much of the evidence drawing on the results of aerial photography.

(i) *Raedykes*

Crawford's consideration of the problem of *Mons Graupius*, incorporated in the published version of the Rhind Lectures delivered in 1943 (Crawford 1949, 128–33), was just too early to make appreciable use of air-photograph evidence, although his final sentence indicates that he foresaw the extent of its eventual contribution. That deficiency was compensated, however, by his first-hand knowledge of the terrain as well as the fact that, although air survey has multiplied the number of marching-camps, it has not widened their distribution much beyond the area of North-eastern Scotland which Crawford would have had in mind. Taking Macdonald's pronouncement on the date of the legionary fortress at Inchtuthil as his starting point, Crawford presumed that in his last campaign Agricola had 'followed the time-honoured route along Strathmore', and he agreed with Stuart Miller that the battle 'must have been at some place which Calgacus knew the Romans must pass in their advance northwards'. The ideal site had to be an open place with a plain adjacent, the Roman camp on one side, and wooded hills on the other; at least one native village had to be in sight and there could have been no rivers of any size in the vicinity, since this would have drawn comment from Tacitus. Such requirements indicated to Crawford that the only reasonable site was Raedykes, situated on a ridge that:

> leads like an open corridor to northern Scotland. It was the obvious way from Strathmore to Aberdeenshire in early days, from Southern to Northern Pictland in the Dark Ages. Here the invader must pass and here he must be stopped before he escapes into the vast spaces beyond, where he can manoeuvre and retain his initiative. (Crawford 1949, 132)

In Crawford's eyes, the Roman camps lying to the north of Raedykes need not have marked the route of the victorious army which Agricola led down (*deducit*), through the territory of the Boresti, to the coast; indeed, if the battle was fought at Raedykes, a long march beyond, possibly as far as the Spey, would seem to represent just such a widening of the area of campaigning which Tacitus claims to have been out of the question. Thus Crawford implies that the construction of the camps from Normandykes northwards might possibly be the work of Agricola's successor, a point which will be taken up later (pp. 115–16).

(ii) *Pass of Grange*

In the first flush of excitement over the results of aerial reconnaissance, as the significance of the Stracathro-gated camps began to be

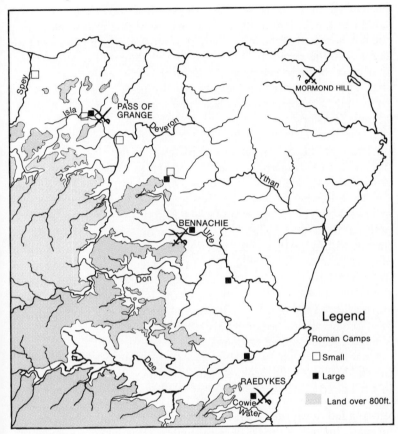

Figure 24. Proposed battle-sites north of the Mounth, showing relationships to presumed first-century Roman camps.

realised, there were several attempts to use air-photograph evidence to identify the site of the battle. The most impressive was that of A. R. Burn (1953b), whose basic thesis was that the discovery of a Stracathro-gated camp at Auchinhove, 3 kilometres north-east of Keith, showed convincingly that military operations of the Flavian period had extended at least to the north of the Mounth and very probably as far as the coast of the Moray Firth; the fact that the battle had been fought late in the season suggested that it took place near the northern end of the long chain of camp-sites which stretched from the Tay to the mouth of the River Spey; although it was recognised that many of these camps might be of Severan origin, Burn argued that later generals would have known from military records of the routes taken by their predecessors and would have tended to follow in their footsteps.

In his attempt to fix on the precise location, Burn introduced the question of the extent of the battlefield, a practical point which no one had satisfactorily considered before. According to Burn, Agricola's extended front (*diductis ordinibus*) of both infantry and cavalry would have required between 2.4 and 3.2 kilometres of open ground, which fact alone would argue against the battle having taken place at Raedykes, where the expanse of level moorland is too narrow; Burn further observed that the heights to the north of Raedykes, where Crawford placed the Caledonian army, were not prominent enough to produce the effect which Tacitus describes of the enemy ranks rising in tiers above the Roman position. In short, Burn rejected the best-argued proposal to have been made thus far, and, in the process, he could have added that Crawford's 'Caledonian Village' is not a native settlement but a cairnfield!

Unable to find any Roman camp site then known that satisfied all the conditions upon which he insisted, Burn selected a position which in his opinion, at least satisfied all the physical requirements, and might possibly straddle a frontier between component elements of the Caledonian confederacy – the tribes of Buchan and Moray respectively. The position (figure 25) lies between Knock Hill and the Pass of Grange, to the east of Keith, and some 4 kilometres east of Auchinhove, where the steep ridge of Sillyearn Hill (*c.*245 m OD) extends south-westwards into Strathisla, combining with the Little Balloch on the opposite side of the valley to constrict the westward passage to a width of barely 1.2 kilometres. Burn suggested that, if this was indeed the position, Agricola's first aim would have been to clear the enemy off the Sillyearn ridge, while the attempted encircling movement by the Caledonians would have been launched from the summit of Knock Hill and the high ground on the south side of the Isla; the prominent conical summit of Knock Hill (430 m OD) was

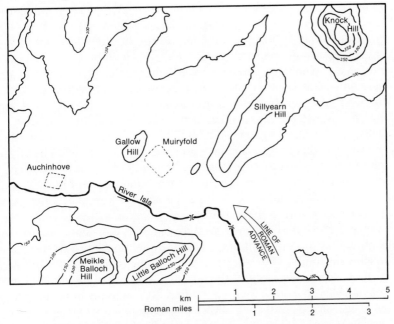

Figure 25. Plan of the battle-site at Pass of Grange, Grampian Region, proposed by Burn and Henderson-Stewart.

also tentatively proposed as the original of *Mons Graupius*, Gaelic *cnoc* (hillock) being equated, at least in meaning, with Old Welsh *crup* (hump). In a later, but briefer, discussion of the battle, Burn (1969, 55–8) added the comment that the chariotry which filled the *media campi* before the two armies got to grips had been stationed in the col between Knock Hill and Sillyearn, but, as observed above (p. 58), it is difficult to see what sense such a disposition made. In both accounts Burn's reading of the strategic issues is the same: Agricola's experience of near disaster in the sixth season had made him particularly sensitive about the security of his communications, while the Caledonians had realised that the redeployment and counter-marching of that year had almost allowed them to break through to the Romans' rear. In the seventh season, therefore, the two armies continued to spar until Agriccla out-manoeuvred Calgacus and 'got his enemy where he wanted them'. The weakness of this line of argument is that Tacitus gives the impression of direct advance to a known and well-prepared position, while the likelihood of a Roman field-force, even *expedito exercitu*, being able to out-think a Caledonian host on its own territory seems extremely remote. Moreover, the fact that the army was *expeditus* surely precludes a long drawn-out operation, while, as has been pointed out elsewhere (Ogilvie and Richmond 1967, 65), 'in British strategy the pre-selected position was something of a habit'; Boudicca, Caratacus, and possibly Venutius appear to have eventually chosen, as did Calgacus, to meet the invader head-on. Certainly, it must be admitted that occupying the Sillyearn ridge did not constitute the best method of evading the enemy's notice and slipping beneath his guard.

It could of course be argued, as Burn did, that Calgacus only stood his ground at the very end of the season, when it seemed likely that the Romans might, after all, penetrate into the rich cornlands of the Laich of Moray; win or lose, the invaders would then have had little time in which to extend their operations. Nevertheless, it seems odd that Calgacus did not then take the opportunity of moving covertly to Agricola's rear, where his presence threatening both the line of communications and the newly occupied lands to the south would surely have shaken the resolution of any Roman commander and persuaded him, without the risk of a major conflict, that the price to be paid for further advance might be unacceptably high.

The above objections to Burn's rather over-subtle interpretation of the strategic context, need not be raised with regard to the selection of the same locality by Henderson-Stewart, whose arguments in favour of its identification as *Mons Graupius* are straightforward: the Pass of Grange was the natural gateway to the Moray Firth and the Caledonian heartlands, it lay close to the most northerly Roman camp then known, and it offered almost the only position along the route from the Dee to the Spey where natural advantages favoured the defender. Henderson-Stewart was further impressed by the gap of approximately 29 kilometres between Auchinhove and Glenmailen and suggests that a 'missing' camp, situated some way to the east of the Pass of Grange, should therefore be sought. Auchinhove was thus interpreted as the camp constructed by Agricola after the battle, its singular appearance (by which the author meant both its size and the possession of Stracathro-type gates), contrasting with that of the nearest 53-hectare sites and thus implying 'some considerable alteration in the circumstances of the Roman army'. Although Henderson-Stewart had little to say that had not already been expressed in Burn's article, and despite his disconcerting references to the Caledonian forces as 'the Scots', two points in particular were well-made: firstly, where a regular marching-interval has been established in a series of camps, any deviation from that pattern, or from the apparent line of march, may be significant; and secondly, when a series of camps mostly of identical area is found to include an example of exceptional size, this too may be deemed significant.

Both versions of the argument in favour of the Pass of Grange were to be seriously weakened, however, by the discovery of a Roman temporary camp, apparently of the 53-hectare series, at Muiryfold on the south-west slope of Gallow Hill (figure 25) barely 2 kilometres east of Auchinhove and immediately to the west of the Sillyearn ridge (St Joseph 1961, 123). Such a camp would certainly have been capable of holding an army as large as Agricola's at *Mons Graupius*, but it would be difficult to see it as the base of a field-force assaulting the Sillyearn-Knock Hill position, unless we imagine the Romans to have been cut off as they retreated from the furthest limit of their advance, an assumption which does not square with either probability or the course of events described by Tacitus. The discovery of the camp did provide an apt illustration of the dangers which have always beset proponents of any particular solution to this intriguing problem, namely that the most judicious consideration of the evidence may be upset, in the twinkling of an eye, by the next happy discovery or insight. Even in archaeology the pace of enlightenment and exploration, especially with the aid of aerial reconnaissance, can be cruelly swift. Nevertheless, the awkward presence of the large camp at Muiryfold made little initial impact upon the favour with which the Burn/Henderson-Stewart theory was looked upon by scholars in general; the locality was still mentioned in terms of approbation by Ogilvie and Richmond (1967, 251–2) and Wellesley (1969a, 268), while Burn himself had seen no reason to change his opinion in a later discussion (1969, 55–8). In fact, the situation did not change until St Joseph showed that the average size of the five large camps north of

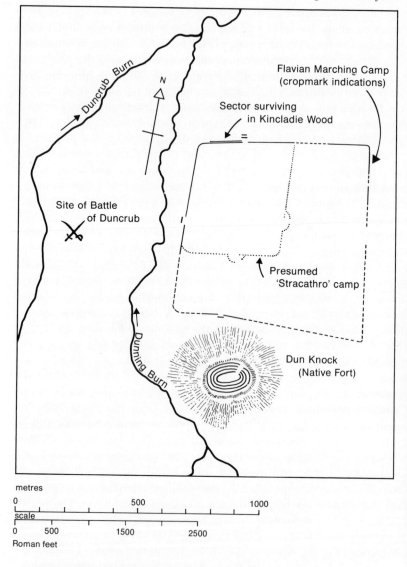

Figure 26. Plans of the proposed battlefield at Dunning, in the valley of the Earn, showing outline of suspected Stracathro-type camp within structure eventually indicated by air photography.

Stonehaven was appreciably less than 53 hectares (1973, 231–3). He therefore suggested that the Severan date hitherto presumed for these sites might, in fact, only apply to the 53-hectare camps south of Stonehaven, the five northernmost camps possibly being the bivouacs of Agricola's army in the seventh campaign. St Joseph supported his contention by pointing to the basic similarity between these sites, which averaged about 45 hectares, and two indubitably Flavian marching-camps at Dunning and Abernethy in the valley of the Earn (pp. 18–19 above), with an average of 47 hectares.

(iii) *Duncrub*

By a strange quirk of fate this comparative material, which in time enabled St Joseph to suggest an even more probable site for *Mons Graupius* (below, p. 105) had been provided by a chain of investigation that sprang from a third, and extremely radical, attempt to pinpoint the great conflict. In an article published to mark the fiftieth anniversary of the appointment of O. G. S. Crawford as first Archaeology Officer in the Ordnance Survey, R. W. Feachem, an eminent successor to that post, argued ingeniously for a site in Kincladie Wood, near Dunning, in Perthshire (1970). First recorded in an anonymous description of the parish of Dunning in 1723 (Mitchell 1906, 121), the site then appeared as a 'Trench' which was 'capable to contain several thousands of men'; when examined by Crawford (1949, 59) only about 130 metres of bank and ditch survived, scarcely enough to permit a definite identification, and Crawford contented himself with the remark 'the possibility that it might be a fragment ot a Roman camp . . . cannot be altogether excluded'. Later inspection of the site during routine map-revision work by officers of the Ordnance Survey led Feachem to suggest that it formed part of a Stracathro-gated temporary camp about 16 ha in area. The circumstance which, in his opinion, charged this fragmentary site with exceptional significance was the proximity of Duncrub Hill (figure 26), a locality that had been philologically equated with *Dorsum Crup* (Watson 1926, 56), the site of a battle between contestants for the Scottish crown in the tenth century AD, and a place-name that might equally well have been latinised as *Mons Craupius* (see above, p. 55). The coincidence of all these elements – camp, place-name and battle-site – not unnaturally made a strong impression on Feachem, and he was persuaded thereby that a radical re-interpretation of the Tacitean account was justified. In particular, it seemed possible that after the attack on the Ninth Legion had been beaten off (*Agricola*, xxvii),

> Agricola *left* strictly Caledonian territory and went north, encountering only scattered *Vacomagi* and *Taezali* and such on his march to the Moray Firth; and that he soon returned (*Agricola*, xxix, 2–4) to resume the fight with the confederate league – which included the *Venicones* (who were to become the influential Maeatae) and was led by the Caledonian chieftain (who might have been a refugee from the south) – at a site selected, because of its importance to themselves, by the British. (Feachem 1970, 122–3)

Feachem also pointed out the proximity of the Pictish and Scottish capital of Forteviot, which has more recently been found to adjoin an extensive complex of prehistoric ritual structures (St Joseph 1978b, 48–50; Alcock 1980, 84–5).

Even as stated, the proposal involved too brutal an interpretation of the text to win widespread approval. But aerial discovery and trial excavation were soon to change fundamentally the perceived character of the earthwork that had inspired the theory. In the same year as Feachem's article was published, Professor St Joseph recorded cropmarks indicating that, while the site was indeed a Roman camp it extended well beyond the limits which had previously been assumed; within three years virtually the whole of the perimeter had been observed and the area assessed at about 47 ha, or roughly three times as great as the first estimate. Moreover, excavation of the sole surviving gateway proved beyond all doubt that the entrance had been protected by a *titulum* and not a *clavicula*. By the curious workings of fate, the same period also brought to light two camps, apparently of comparable area, the first situated one, the second two days' march to the east. The nearest of these, at Abernethy, was dated to the late 1st century by the South Gaulish samian found in its ditch, and a similar date was argued for the other, at Carpow, because of its structural relationship to a presumed Severan work and the disposition of its entrance (St Joseph 1973, 219–23). It thus seemed reasonable to interpret all three camps as evidence of an Agricolan force moving eastwards towards the south bank of the Tay,

Figure 27. Air photograph of area to the south of Dunning, showing curvilinear cropmarks of multivallate native hillfort on Dun Knock (top left) and the line of cropmark above the south ditch of the Roman marching camp (to right of road).

rather than westwards to an appointment with destiny. Ironically, a year or two later, aerial survey revealed evidence (figure 27) of a multivallate native fort crowning the prominent hill immediately to the south of Dunning camp. It now seems possible that this was the fort or 'dun' referred to in the place-name Duncrub, which by its late discovery narrowly missed a short-lived fame as *Mons Graupius*.

The series of three to which Dunning belonged, moreover, could be connected with the group of large camps between Raedykes and Muiryfold (St Joseph 1973, 231–1). It was argued that the camps between Dunning and Carpow might indicate the early progress of a Flavian force which had crossed the Tay at Carpow and then made its way up the coast of Angus towards Stonehaven; to the south of the Tay it would thus have re-used camps originally constructed in Agricola's third campaign (*usque ad Taum aestuarium*), or possibly in the sixth season, before the Caledonian surprise attack. St Joseph's reason for advocating their secondary occupation was the need to show how the force occupying the northernmost camps had proceeded to the Mounth without otherwise leaving a trace of their march, for some six marching-intervals would have been required between the putative crossing at Carpow and the camp at Raedykes. Furthermore, the discovery of what appeared to be a camp exceeded 20 hectares in area, at Logie, where the proposed line of march might have conveniently crossed the River North Esk, seemed to confirm that in time, the five missing intermediate bivouac-sites would be recognised.

(iv) *Bennachie*

In 1975, in the course of a reconnaissance flight from Scone to the Moray Firth (St Joseph 1978a), approximately half the perimeter of a large Roman camp was recorded by St Joseph at Durno about 10 kilometres north-west of Inverurie (figure 28). Later survey and excavation proved it to be the largest temporary camp in Northern Scotland, at least 57 hectares in area. Yet its exceptional size was of less significance than its situation, for it occupied a roughly medial position between the 44-hectare camps at Ythan Wells and Kintore and was 'set forward, that is to the west, 1.5 kilometres from the straight line joining the two.' (St Joseph 1978a, 278). Durno lay not far distant from the point at which the direction of movement, as indicated by the large camp-sites, inclined from a generally north-ward direction towards the northwest, the alteration taking place 'not far from the confluence of the Urie and the Don and opposite the distinctive granite mountain of Bennachie'. St Joseph then pointed out that the area of the camp at Durno (57 hectares) equalled the sum of the areas of the Stracathro-gated type of camp from the same area and the other large sites, 44 hectares and 13 hectares. He had already (1973, 232) given reason for believing that the interval which elapsed

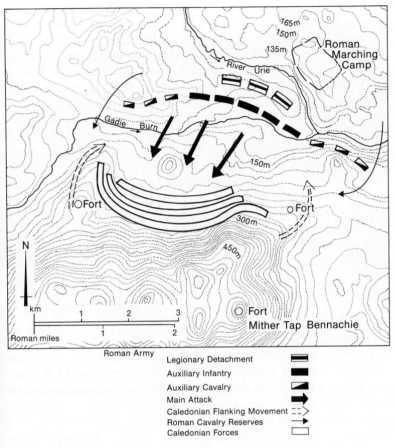

Roman Army
Legionary Detachment
Auxiliary Infantry
Auxiliary Cavalry
Main Attack
Caledonian Flanking Movement
Roman Cavalry Reserves
Caledonian Forces

Figure 28. The suggested course of action fought at Durno-Bennachie (after St Joseph).

between the excavation of the Stracathro camp and the building of the superimposed 44-hectare work at Ythan Wells was almost negligible, although the same evidence had earlier been interpreted as confirming a gap of more than a century. It was now possible to suggest that the two types of camp had accommodated two normally independent forces engaged in the same campaign, which had been

Figure 29. Aerial view of the Durno battlefield, looking south towards the peaked profile of Bennachie.

united to deal with some exceptional situation. The nature of the latter was explained by the proximity to Bennachie: it was *Mons Graupius* (figure 29).

Few candidates for this honour have satisfied so many of the criteria that have been proposed from time to time. Bennachie has a distinctive and unmistakable profile, visible from several directions for a considerable distance, affording the natural advantages of a strongly defensible position, as well as guarding a natural line of movement from Buchan into the Laich of Moray. It is large enough to have been used as a place of assembly by an army many thousands strong and it bears upon two of its summits vestiges of fortified enclosures, which, like the numerous comparable sites on adjacent hills, demonstrate that the area was a focus for settlement, if not in the Roman period, at least at a date not utterly remote from it. There was, moreover, ample space for the arraying of a Roman line of battle which may have extended for more than 2.5 kilometres, without cramping the movement of cavalry disposed on the wings, while the north front of Bennachie opposite the Roman camps presents the steeply sloping concave face necessary to give the impression of towering heights packed with Caledonian warriors. In fact, a detailed exposition of the various phases of the engagement can be made to show (figure 28) how well the terrain at Bennachie-Durno accommodates the action described by Tacitus: the position of the Roman camp, well down the south-west slope of a local eminence, effectively opposes it to the Bennachie massif and at the same time brings within easy reach the River Urie, a minor tributary of the Don, but an adequate source of water even for so large a force as Agricola's; the Roman battle-line could thus be drawn up on the far, i.e. the southern, side of the Urie, without being too far removed from the bivouac's protection, and without having to cross the stream to come to grips with the enemy – a relatively slight obstacle, but one which might otherwise have merited a reference in the description of the battle; the terrain at the foot of Bennachie, though hardly to be described as a level plain, is nevertheless extensive enough to permit the cavortings of British chariotry, while the rock-strewn upper slopes of the northern face, curving round the ground over which the Roman *auxilia* would have had to advance, represent an ideally strong defensive position, where it would be difficult for cavalry to operate and from which even infantry would have laboured to dislodge the enemy. St Joseph notes 'the advantage to the Romans of drawing the Caledonian forces down from the steeper ground' (1978a, 284), and, whether engineered by Agricola or not, this is precisely what the Caledonians did (*Agricola*, xxxvii, 1), although not till a late stage in the battle; once again, the form of the mountain, with eastern and western ridges offering a relatively easy means of descent on either flank, lends itself to such an enveloping manoeuvre.

Even the rout and aftermath of the battle fit appropriately into the environs of Bennachie, the stricken warriors and kinsmen fleeing in disorder over the watershed into the valley of the Don and hence into the hidden refuge of the mountain ranges lying to the west. The Roman troops left in possession of the field might gaze in wonder over the rolling plains of Buchan and see nothing but the palls of smoke that marked the locations of deserted settlements, and turning to the Grampian massif, hear only the windy echoes of the highland hills. The subsequent progress of the main Roman battle group, the smaller unit having for some reason reverted to operating independently, would then be indicated by the larger camp at Ythan Wells and Muiryfold; the relatively short interval between Durno and the next camp to the north-west, only 11.7 kilometres, might be cited as evidence of the slow pace (*lento itinere*) adopted by Agricola after the victory, as he proceeded through the territory of the *Boresti* towards the sea. Finally, the reader is directed to consider the possibility of locating caches of military equipment, the ideal location being between the Urie and Gagie Burn, where aerial reconnaisance might at some time in the future reveal the existence of tell-tale pits. When these have been found, it is claimed, the criteria for the recognition of Bennachie as *Mons Graupius* and Durno as the camp of Agricola's army will have been adequately met. In this, as in all other cases, to adopt St Joseph's words, 'readers will form their own judgement'; but the evidence is formidably persuasive.

It must be remembered, nevertheless, that one of the paths by which St Joseph had proceeded to this identification was the presumption that Agricola's advance to Bennachie had been by way of the coastal route, which involved a crossing of the Tay at Carpow and the North Esk at Logie. Unfortunately, by 1977 linear cropmarks at the latter site had been found to be of recent agricultural origin, while both the Flavian date and precise nature of the work at Carpow still await verification, despite continuing intensive aerial inspection of the site. Nor has aerial survey succeeded in locating even one of the coastal camps presumed to lie between the Tay and Raedykes. It still has to be satisfactorily explained, therefore, how Agricola's 'grand army' reached the Mounth without apparently leaving a trace of its progress. Recent discussion (Maxwell 1980, 28–9,–40), moreover, has drawn attention to the elongated rectangular plan exhibited by most of the large camps between Muiryfold and the Mounth, which contrast with the tendency for Flavian sites to favour square plan-form – the camps at Dunning and Abernethy representing good examples of the latter. It may still reasonably be asked why these northern examples should necessarily be sundered from the series of camps between Ardoch and Kair House, whose line of march they so aptly extend and whose structural proportions they so closely reproduce. St Joseph answered this question by enquiring in turn (1978a, 278) how the series of 53-hectare camps, designed to accommodate an Imperial expedition to the remotest limits of Britain, could have been reduced in area by 8 hectares when the troops were operating at their greatest distance from base, and hence in the most dangerous phase of the campaign. Yet he himself was happy to explain the 6.5-hectare difference between Raedykes and the majority of the 'Agricolan' camps north of the Mounth as the result of its proximity to Stonehaven, where a small force, detached from the main body, could have been required to guard and maintain a coastal stores base or transhipment point.

It may be useful to consider at this point the nature of the camp at Raedykes (figure 10), the irregularity of whose plan sets it apart from other camps in northern Scotland. Its position, too, is far from the type which Roman military manuals identified as desirable (Hyginus *de munitionibus*, 54, 58), and Sir George Macdonald himself described it (1916, 318) as 'one which a Roman general would hardly have occupied except under stress of circumstances'. It would be interesting to speculate what these circumstances were, for the reduction in effective area of Raedykes would appear to have resulted mainly from slipshod surveying: the length and maximum width of the camp, about 805 metres and 635 metres respectively, approximate to the axial dimensions of the average Severan 53-hectare site. Furthermore, if one could be sure that the detached length of ditch and rampart lying some 100 metres to the south was also of Roman military construction, as Crawford suggested (1949, 108–10), it would not be unreasonable to argue that in the initial stages this was intended to serve as the southernmost limit of a camp measuring roughly 900 metres by 635 metres, which closely approaches the axial dimensions of Durno itself (*c.* 930 metres by 605 metres). It can thus be seen that the argument in favour of identifying Bennachie as *Mons Graupius* should not lean too heavily on the morphology of temporary camps.

One of the main criticisms of St Joseph's suggested dispositions (1978, fig. 7) is that, unless the Roman lines were drawn up dangerously far from the protection of the marching-camp, the distance between the two armies would seem to have been inconveniently great. Considering that only 600 metres separated the opposing sides at Culloden, or between 300 and 1000 metres at Agincourt, the interval of at least 1800 metres that extended from the front line of the *auxilia* to the nearest of the Caledonian warriors, at the foot of the concave north face of Bennachie, must surely be out of the question for armies that lacked the support of long-range missiles such as cannon, musket, or even longbow; the problems of co-ordinating the movements of the various Roman units would also have been enormously increased as they advanced further and further from the *vexilla*, the ensigns of the legionary detachments, in front of which Agricola had, in modern parlance, set up his command-post. The other respect in which the described battlefield seems too large for the combatants is the vastness of the Bennachie massif upon which Calgacus' warriors were deployed. The entire Jacobite army at Culloden probably occupied no more than 30 ha of Drummossie Moor, despite the fact that its 5000 foot and horse were generously spaced; at Bennachie even an army six times as strong would have found it difficult to cover the area of between 500 and 600 ha indicated by St Joseph and still give the impression of serried ranks that so impressed Agricola. It is, of course, quite possible that the battlefield covered a much smaller portion of Bennachie, for example only the lower slopes, but to pursue this line of argument would perhaps be to admit that Bennachie does not in fact possess the peculiar advantages of terrain which recommend it exclusively as the site of *Mons Graupius*.

The above list, of course, does not exhaust the range of possibilities that have been considered, and continue to be proposed, for the site of the battlefield. The claim that the Romans penetrated the lands to the west of the River Spey continues to be made, as is perfectly acceptable. Sites near Elgin and Inverness have recently been examined as evidence of Agricolan permanent occupation north of the Grampians (Jones 1986; Keillar 1986), and the location of *Mons Graupius* nearer to Cape Wrath than Central Scotland can also be rationally discussed (Henderson 1984). Still more recently, the attractive qualities of Duncrub have been discussed afresh (Smith 1987) without, however, producing tangible evidence. In short, there is no sign that the appetite for the Grampian quest is seriously diminished.

SIX

The Epilogue

MOST people would agree with the reviewer of a recent study of Agricola's achievements in North Britain (Jarrett 1982) that 'Scottish antiquarian literature will be the poorer, and Scottish topography less well studied if the battlefield is ever found'; and, one must add, archaeology will be deprived of one of its more engaging sideshows. Happily, it would seem that such a time has not yet arrived. Even if it had, there would remain the task of relating the episode of final conquest to the years of consolidation and occupation which followed. The evidence for the latter, as has recently been made clear (Breeze 1980; Frere 1980), is still capable of widely divergent interpretations, a state of affairs which invites at least brief examination, in the hope that an appreciation of the later Flavian permanent dispositions in Scotland north of the Forth may cast some light on the campaigning that went immediately before.

Regardless of the differing dates assigned to them by different scholars, the various categories of Flavian frontier works appear to be at least dual in character (figure 30): the permanent forts may be subdivided (Hanson 1980a, 28–30; 1987, 143–58) into a main-route group comprising those which guard the road from Stirling to the Tay as well as those sited in the central valley of Strathmore, and an outer *limes* group (sometimes called 'glen-blocking' forts), set forward against the very edge of the Highland Line from Drumquhassle to Fendoch. This latter group could have been intended to screen the legionary fortress at Inchtuthil, whose establishment might be the work of Agricola's successor. The existence of a chain of watch-towers along the Gask Ridge, between Strageath and the Tay, extending southwards from Strageath to Ardoch (and possibly beyond) has seemed to some (e.g. Breeze and Dobson 1976, 129–31; Breeze, 1982, 61–5) incompatible with the manning of the outer *limes*

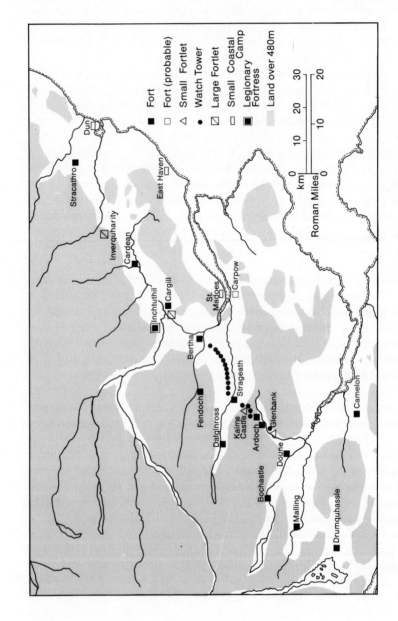

Figure 30 Flavian garrisons in Strathmore and possible coastal 'provisioning points'.

orts, and it has been presumed that when Inchtuthil was abandoned n *c.* AD 86 or 87, the screening forts were also given up, leaving the watch-tower line with its adjacent forts as the effective northern frontier of the province. Within a few years even this reduced area of occupation was evacuated and by AD 90 Roman garrisons had been withdrawn well to the south of the Forth (cf. Hanson and Maxwell 1983, 44–7). On the other hand Frere (1980a, 94–7) has argued cogently that 'the pattern if not all the details of the Flavian fort-system in Scotland north of the Forth was in existence' by the end of Agricola's seventh campaign.

In the present state of knowledge it is impossible to distinguish by archaeological means between the works of AD 80–84 and those of AD 84–7. It is nevertheless clear that an appreciable degree of structural development or change occurred on individual sites and within the system generally. The existence of both a fort *and* fortlet at Cargill, guarding the crossing of the Isla east of Inchtuthil, and the possibility that the fortlet at Inverquharity, near Kirriemuir, complements a major fort at Finavon (Maxwell and Wilson 1987, 15–16, 21–22), may well betoken two distinct phases of frontier development; the second presumably coincides with the integration of the legionary fortress in the northern *limes* (Pitts and St Joseph 1985, 273–8). Even within the series of watch-towers of the Doune-Ardoch-Bertha 'frontier' (Maxwell 1989b), there are variations of plan and disposition which appear to indicate two separate approaches to the problem. Those to the south of the River Earn appear to be set mainly within two very slight circular ditches and separated from each other by a relatively regular interval of almost 1000 metres; those to the north were, for the most part, protected by a single broad ditch and occasionally a turf rampart, while the intervening distances vary from about 760 to 1520 metres.

It is tempting to compare this evidence with a similar pattern in the categories of temporary works, in particular with the complementary patterns of distribution exhibited by marching-camps of the 53–58-ha group and those of the smaller, Stracathro-gated type (above, pp. 51–4). It can be argued, for example, that the series of extremely large camps which extends from Raedykes to Muiryfold, but is represented by no example between Raedykes and the Tay, relates to campaigning carried out by Agricola's successor.

There is no explicit historical evidence of post-Agricolan campaigning in the later 1st century AD, and Tacitus observes that Agricola handed over to his successor a province that was both secure and peaceful (*Agricola*, xl, 3). Yet we know that in his last campaign Agricola had been prevented from exploiting his victory to the full by the approach of winter. Would it not have been natural for the incoming governor to 'tie up the loose ends'? To a large extent this depends on the date of Agricola's departure from Britain, and just how much time was left to the next governor to develop his plans for the northern frontier before the crescendo of military pressures on the Rhine and Danube made it necessary once more to move troops out of the province to serve on the Continent. For example, the *Legio II Adiutrix* had been withdrawn to Moesia certainly by AD 92–3 and perhaps as early as AD 86–7, its departure being followed or possibly even preceded, by the transfer of the Twentieth Legion from Inchtuthil to Chester (cf. Frere 1978, 116–18; Pitts and St Joseph 1985, 279–81); both transfers would also have been attended by a relocation of auxiliary troops, additionally depleting the forces available for deployment, in any capacity, on the northern frontier.

Early dating of Agricola's governorship allows us to associate the sweeping advances of the third campaign (*usque ad Taum*) with the Emperor Titus' fifteenth imperatorial acclamation, which occurred in AD 79 (Birley 1981, 80). Accordingly, Titus would have died at the end of Agricola's fifth campaign, and as Dobson has observed (1981, 10), it would harmonise the two seasons of military consolidation with the years in which Titus alone was responsible for imperial policy decisions. With Domitian's accession in September 81, the credit for approving the further advances of the sixth and seventh campaigns in 82 and 83 respectively may be safely assigned to the new emperor. Ogilvie and Richmond (1967, 319–20), however, argue that the date of Domitian's triumph following a victory won over the Chatti and the character of coins commemorating his seventh acclamation support the acceptance of the later dating of *Mons Graupius*. Since the Chattan triumph did not take place till late in 83, it has generally been thought unlikely that, if Agricola's victory over Calgacus had occurred in the same year, Tacitus could have represented Domitian hearing no news of it until after the ludicrous stage management of his own triumph (*conscientia derisui fuisse uper falsum e Germania triumphum*). It has also been suggested that he coins of Domitian's seventh acclamation, which show a Roman avalryman riding down a barbarian, constitute a direct reference to he manner in which the battle of *Mons Graupius* was won. Since the battle did not take place until summer was past (*exacta iam aestate*), nd the fleet was in the vicinity of the Orkneys when winter was pproaching (*Agricola*, x, 4), it is unlikely that news could have been rought to Rome of the successful termination of operations on land nd sea before the beginning of December (cf. Birley 1981, 78–9). Reports of successful events in Britain would then have followed hard n the heels of Domitian's mock triumph, and Tacitus' use of *nuper* vould have been even more appropriate than if the victory had been von in 84 and 'recently' represented an interval of more than a year. The attempt to link Domitian's seventh acclamation with the victory t *Mons Graupius* can be rebutted on two counts, for, in the first place, the acclamation is recorded on a military diploma from ²annonia (CIL, XVI, 30) dated 3 September 84, far too soon after he end of the campaigning season for it to be a reference to Agricola's victory, had it indeed occurred in that year; and secondly, he cavalry motif that appears on the reverse of the coins associated vith that acclamation is by no means so rare a type of battle composition as Ogilvie and Richmond claimed – it figures for example on three of the Distance Slabs from the Antonine Wall (cf. Keppie 1979, nos. 1 and 6) – and although it might conceivably be used to illustrate the sort of battle which Agricola fought (cf. Robertson 1975, 367) the connection remains unproven.

If the battle of *Mons Graupius* was fought in the early autumn of AD 83, the army of Britain could thereafter have enjoyed at least two years in which to prosecute a policy of expansion undiminished by the transfer of troops to the Continent. Frere has suggested (1980a, 92) that the existence of a full complement of legionary barracks at Inchtuthil shows that the vexillations sent to Germany to support Domitian's campaign in the Wetterau had returned soon after the Chattan triumph in late 83. Until Oppius Sabinus was defeated and killed by the Dacians who invaded Moesia in 85, therefore, it is probable that Agricola's successor in the provincial governorship commanded an army stronger even than that engaged at *Mons Graupius*. Consequently, it is possible to argue that in 84 the occupation of Strathmore was either taken in hand or completed, and in the same year, or the next, field-forces operated once more, or conceivably for the first time, north of the Mounth, thoroughly rooting out the last vestiges of resistance and ensuring that the zone lying immediately outside the limits of the province would not provide a hotbed of disaffection to trouble tribesmen who lived under the *pax Romana* to the south. There is no reference in Roman literature to the regime which succeeded Agricola's, but even had it been the occasion for further campaigning and conquest, we would not expect Tacitus to have mentioned it, since this would have diminished the lustre of Agricola's laurels. Equally, we can be sure that his successor did not preside over the dismemberment of Agricola's northern conquests, for Tacitus would have been swift to impute this to imperial jealousy or mismanagement.

When reviewing the fortunes of the provinces under Domitian in a later work (*Histories*, i, 2) Tacitus coined the memorable statement *perdomita Britannia et statim omissa* ('Britain was completely conquered and then immediately forgotten about'). As Macdonald argued (1937) and as archaeology has confirmed, *omissa* represents a process of neglect, and not abrupt abandonment, extended over almost two decades.

Does this necessarily affect the identification of the site of *Mons Graupius*? In the sense that we may no longer need to regard the northernmost temporary structures of presumed Flavian date as inevitably the work of Agricola, the answer is yes; but whether that means we should look for *Mons Graupius* further to the south cannot yet be determined. At the very least, such considerations may persuade us to look again at the premises upon which we build our theories about the Agricolan campaigns, and if that leads to a more critical examination of both the topography and archaeology of Scotland north of the Tay, no harm will be done. It is possible that there exist clues which we have not yet recognised, and it may be appropriate to mention an example.

Ptolemy's *Geography* contains a reference (II, 3, 7) to a *polis*, or occupied site, called *Victoria*; the same place-name is listed in the *Ravenna Cosmography* (108, 11) in the locative form *Victorie*. It is described by Ptolemy as situated amongst the *Dumnonii*, a tribal group which appears to have extended from Ayrshire into southern Perthshire; the map-coordinates given by Ptolemy would place it roughly between Forth and Tay. Traditionally and even in modern times, the name has been associated with the scene of the foiled assault upon the Ninth Legion (Ogilvie and Richmond 1967, 243–4), but a recent study of place-names in Roman Britain (Rivet and Smith 1979, 499) has proposed that it should be equated with Inchtuthil, on the grounds that the fortress was occupied by the *Legio XX Victrix*. Still more recently, however, it has been pointed out (Frere 1980b, 421) that such an identification is extremely improbable, since the adjective derived from *Victrix* would be *Victricensis*. The most suitable place-name for Inchtuthil to appear in Ptolemy's list is *Pinnata Castra*, which should be translated as 'the fortress with stone merlons (crenellated walls)', a reference to the handsome masonry of Strathmore conglomerate with which the legionary base's ramparts were once revetted. Unfortunately, Ptolemy's *Pinnata* is located amongst the *Vacomagi* and assigned map-coordinates which place it somewhere between the Rivers Spey and Lossie and no great distance from the south shore of the Moray Firth. Apart from the near certain identification with Inchtuthil, *Pinnata* is one of the six sites in Britain for which Ptolemy offers a measurement of the longest day; if this is genuine, it would have been much more feasible for a permanently occupied base like Inchtuthil, than what Rivet and Smith identify as a temporary camp in the wilds of Caledonia (1979, 440–1).

The inference which may be drawn from such evidence is that, although defined in impressively scientific terms by map-coordinates, the positions of many of Ptolemy's Scottish *poleis*, most, if not all, of which were estimated during the Flavian occupation of North Britain, are far from trustworthy. It is possible, therefore, that as Rivet and Smith imply of the relationship between tribes and *poleis* in the southern parts of Britain (1979, 120–1), the relationships between the named places or tribal areas and the more accurately surveyed coastline may be quite arbitrary; in other words, the locations may have been copied from freehand insertion upon an original map-source, their position being translated into coordinates for ease of transference. The northerly location of *Pinnata* in Ptolemy is thus no argument against an actual situation on the Tay, nor is the attribution of *Victoria* to the *Dumnonii* a satisfactory reason for locating it no further north than southern Perthshire.

Accordingly, it may not be excessively optimistic to suggest that

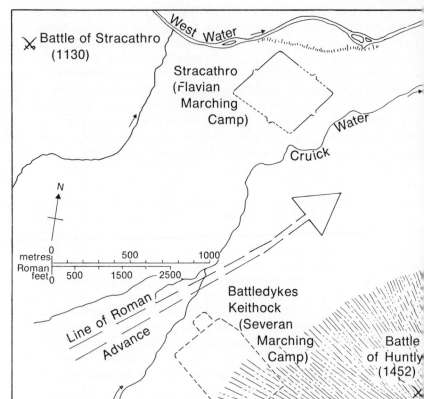

Figure 31a. Sketch-plan of possible battle-site, at Stracathro near Edzell, the scene of conflicts in later times.

Victoria should be identified with a permanently occupied fort near the site of the most outstanding victory obtained by the Romans in their campaigns against Caledonian tribes during the Flavian period. Such an identification would have the interesting consequence that *Mons Graupius* lay within the area eventually occupied by Rome. At present, the most northerly permanent work to be discovered is the fort at Stracathro on the North Esk, but there may also have been a fort somewhere on the Bervie Water, and a coastal site at Stonehaven is not entirely out of the question. In that case, our thoughts would have to turn once more to the tactical issues raised by General Roy and some of the earlier antiquaries. Positions such as Hill of Bruxie, overlooking the road that links Stonehaven with the Mearns, would merit reconnaissance for traces of a temporary camp and adjacent *castellum*, although the permanent fort-site might well lie at some distance, acquiring its name because it commanded a view of the battlefield. High on the list, too, would be the area round Monboddo to the south-west of Glenbervie, where the modern highway to Aberdeen crosses the turbulent Bervie Water. Or perhaps, if Stracathro represents the most northerly outpost of the Roman world, we should look even further south; for it could be argued that the Cairn o' Mounth route, offering an easy passage from the middle reaches of the Don into the Howe of the Mearns would have compromised the security of any garrisons set forward of the River North Esk. In that case, should one look for a site in the vicinity of Edzell, where, in the early medieval period, there were several bloody encounters (figure 31a)? Or is it even possible that the most recent discovery, the Roman fort at Inverquharity on the South Esk to the north east of Kirriemuir, furnishes a still more pregnant clue? Apart from being located near an area which Roy (1793, 85–6) considered the sort of position that Calgacus might have chosen to occupy – the Cat Law massif between Glen Prosen and Glenisla – the new fort represents a divergence from the expected pattern. It lies roughly halfway between the forts of Cardean and Stracathro, but is set forward, that is to the north-west, right against the face of the Grampian massif, guarding the mouths of Glen Prosen and Glen Clova. It is not clear why the Romans did not choose a site on the South Esk closer to the main valley of Strathmore, at Tannadice, for example, where a fort has long been sought, and the presence of temporary camps points to a crossing in Roman times. For the moment it may suffice to comment that the divergence of siting makes an interesting comparison with the situation at Durno-Bennachie; there is little else in its favour.

If the battle of *Mons Graupius* was indeed fought to the south of the Mounth, closer inspection should perhaps be made of locations in or near the Mearns, as Roy suggested. There are various reasons for this, which have been recognised, although differently applied, by most of those who have been engaged on the quest. The battlefield was chosen by Calgacus to ensure a final confrontation and it would therefore overlook or straddle the route that Agricola had to follow; it seems likely that it would also have lain on or near a frontier between two tribal areas and probably some way north of the Tay, although it need not have been utterly remote from it. From what has been said of the native background to Agricola's later campaigns (above, pp. 46–51) it will be realised that the Mearns would meet the latter requirements, while consideration of the routes followed by a succession of armies, from the campaigns of Edward I to the relentless pursuit of the Jacobite army by Cumberland (Maxwell 1984), reveals that, in their northward progress, most have elected to follow the route past Drumlithie and Stonehaven. The Mearns has thus long served as the cockpit of north-east Scotland, well meriting the cognomen of *Claideom* (the Swordland) which it bore in the tenth century (Watson 1926, 110).

As for one specific site, one could do worse than accept Roy's indication of the vicinity of Monboddo, where the elongated, east-west aligned ridge of Knock Hill (figure 31b) stands sentinel opposite Kair House, above the crossing of the Bervie Water. Though rising to a height of only 218 m OD, Knock Hill commands extensive views far down into Strathmore, and in a dry and dusty summer the slow advance of Roman columns might be monitored long before they crossed the North Esk some 25 kilometres, or two days' march, to the south-west; in both form and size it would have been appropriate for the massing of Caledonian levies, its steep southern flank presenting a concave face on which the native host would have towered above Agricola's line in the manner described by Tacitus. There is moreover, ample space for the deployment of chariotry, cavalry, and Roman infantry in extended line, the relatively level shelf to the north of Castleton and Monboddo House being the scene of the initial phases of the battle, while the marching-camp and the legionary detachments could have lain immediately to the south. Thus when drawn up for battle, the respective front-lines need nowhere have been more than 500 metres apart.

As recent archaeological survey has shown (RCAHMS 1982), the

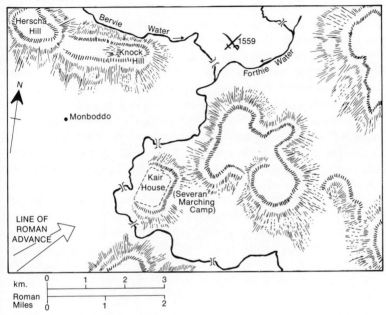

Figure 31b. Sketch of possible battle-site at the crossing of the Bervie Water.

area was comparatively densely occupied in the last three millennia BC, and although there is less evidence of settlement in the Roman Iron Age, we may be reasonably sure that the nearby unenclosed villages of round timber houses, revealed by air survey at Pittengardner and Fordoun, were not isolated examples. An additional point in favour of Knock Hill, apart from its name and appearance, which would accord well with the *crwb* = hump interpretation (above, p. 55), is its proximity to the coast; as a consequence, communication with the fleet would not have presented the same degree of difficulty that must have arisen if the battle had been fought at the inland site of Durno-Bennachie. Where, for example, could the fleet have safely ridden at anchor while waiting for the outcome of the struggle? From Knock Hill a march of only 19 kilometres would have brought Agricola to the shores of the Montrose Basin, where an extensive and sheltered anchorage was assured, and where the existence of a small coastal camp of Flavian date (St Joseph 1973, 225–6) demonstrates that its value as a transhipment point had in fact been appreciated. (Other coastal sites, possibly serving similar purposes, have been noted: St Madoes on the north shore of the Tay estuary and the recently discovered camp at East Haven, between Arbroath and Carnoustie, the former has, until now, been identified as a Severan bridgehead site, but could well have been earlier.) The journey from Knock Hill to the Basin would also aptly illustrate in two senses the use of *deducit* by Tacitus, since it would emphasise what Tacitus expressly states, that Agricola did not extend his operations after *Mons Graupius* but re-traced his steps; such an interpretation is less forced than having to suppose that Tacitus' account could represent a round trip from Bennachie of more than 100 kilometres to the mouth of the Spey and back – even assuming that the fleet would have wished to linger so long in such an exposed situation. It must be stressed, however, that no evidence has yet been recovered of a Roman camp nearer to Knock Hill than Kair House, and the risks of proceeding beyond the North Esk have already been indicated. As a fall-back position, one might therefore nominate a locality to the south of the Esk, possibly on the low hill overlooking Stracathro (Maxwell 1989b). In that case, it would be reasonable, if unconventional, to identify Stracathro as *Victoria* itself!

In conclusion, wherever the battle was fought, we may ask whether *Mons Graupius* deserves to occupy a pre-eminent place in the history of Roman Britain. Has its importance been inflated out of all proportion by the requirements of a literary genre, or by the personal and political aims of the author of the *Agricola*? Historians and the reading public in general tend to prefer a 'decisive' battle, and 'battle reporting' through the ages has obscured the context of every conflict by concentrating on emotive rhetoric and literary impact (Keegan 1976, 34–6, 58–62). All these influences may be seen at work in the *Agricola* (cf. Wellesley 1969b), yet even if they were absent it would be impossible to assess the significance of the battle on the testimony of one side alone. Of the effect which this defeat had on the tribes who rallied to Calgacus there is practically no archaeological evidence – merely a hint that the manufacture of certain types of glass bead in north-east Scotland may have ceased about this time (Guido

1978, 87–9); those who made the ultimate sacrifice deserve a worthier memorial. For any further assessment of the character or results of Agricola's campaigns we must therefore depend on such external evidence as can be provided about Roman military sites by the excavator and aerial surveyor. Yet this, too, as has been shown, may not easily be related to the events described by Tacitus, for it is sometimes difficult to interpret even on its own. All that we can say for certain is that a number of Roman military installations were built in Scotland north of the Forth at about the time that Julius Agricola was governor of Britain, but whether as a direct or indirect result of his achievements cannot be determined. The task is not made any easier by the knowledge that, if a single year's air reconnaissance can still add as many as three forts to the Flavian *limes* (Maxwell 1984b), the quality of our data-base is not particularly high.

This at least can be said: the advances made by the Romans in North Britain in the decade before AD 87 represent one of the most successful series of military operations in the entire history of the province, to which recent minimalist interpretations do scant justice. The exceptional worth of Agricola's contribution to this success may be recognised, if only intuitively, through the stylised eulogies of his son-in-law. Part of that contribution, possibly a large part, was his conduct at *Mons Graupius*, and consequently those who continue to seek the location of the battlefield, or interest themselves in the quest, must ultimately accept the Tacitean verdict: *quantum ad gloriam, longissimum aevum peregit*. It should not be forgotten, however, that the Roman victory was paid for in Caledonian blood, and it is surely to the gallant defenders of North British independence that we owe the ongoing search.

Bibliography

Alcock, L. (1980) 'Populi bestiales Pictorum feroci animo'; a Survey of Pictish Settlement Archaeology, in Hanson and Keppie 1980, 61–96.

Barclay, R. (1777) On Agricola's engagement with the Caledonians, under their leader, Galgacus, *Archaeologia Scotica* 1, 565–70.

Birley, A. R. (1976) The date of Mons Graupius, *Liverpool Classical Monthly 1* no. 2, 11–14.

Birley, A. R. (1981) *The Fasti of Roman Britain*, Oxford.

Breeze, D. J. (1980) Agricola the builder, *Scottish Archaeol. Forum 12*, 14–24.

——(1982) *The Northern Frontiers of Roman Britain*. London.

Breeze, D. J. & B. Dobson (1976) A view of Roman Scotland, *Glasgow Archaeol. J. 4*, 124–43.

Breeze, D. J., J. Close-Brooks & J. N. G. Ritchie (1976) Soldiers' burials at Camelon, Stirlingshire, 1922 and 1975, *Britannia 7*, 73–95.

Buchan, David, 11th Earl of (1786) Remarks on the progress of the Roman arms in Scotland, *Bibliotheca Topographica Britannica 36* vol. 3, appendix, 157.

Burn, A. R. (1953a) *Agricola and Roman Britain*. London.

——(1953b) In search of a battlefield: Agricola's last battle, *Proc. Soc. Antiq. Scotland 87*, 127–33.

——(1969a) Tacitus on Britain, in Dorey 1969, 35–62.

——(1969b) Holy men on islands in pre-Christian Britain, *Glasgow Archaeol. J. 1*, 2–6.

Campbell, D. B. (1985) The consulship of Agricola, *Zeitschrift für Papyrologie und Epigraphik 63*, 197–200.

Chalmers, G. (1807) *Caledonia: or an Account, Historical and Topographic of North Britain*. London.

Crawford, O. G. S. (1930) Editorial notes, *Antiquity 4*, 273–7.

——(1939) Air Reconnaissance of Roman Scotland, *Antiquity 13*, 280–92.

——(1949) *Topography of Roman Scotland North of the Antonine Wall*. Cambridge.

Curle, J. (1911) *A Roman Frontier Post and its People: the Fort of Newstead*. Glasgow.

Davies, R. W. (1970) The Roman military medical service, *Saalburg Jahrbuch 27*, 84–104.

Degrassi, A. (1950) *I Fasti Consolari dell' Imperio Romano*. Rome.

Dobson, B. (1980) Agricola's life and career, *Scottish Archaeol. Forum 12*, 1–13.

Dorey, T. A. (ed.) (1969) *Tacitus*. London.

Douglas, F. (1782) *A General Description of the East Coast of Scotland from Edinburgh to Cullen*. Paisley.

Downey, R. R. (1980) *A History of Archaeological Air Photography in Great Britain (Orbit* 1). London.

Feachem, R. W. (1970) Mons Graupius = Duncrub?, *Antiquity 44*, 120–4.

Frere, S. S. (1978) *Britannia: a history of Roman Britain* (2nd edn). London.

——(1980a) The Flavian frontier in Scotland, *Scottish Archaeol. Forum 12*, 89–97.

——(1980b) Review of Rivet and Smith (1979), in *Britannia 11*, 419–23.

Furneaux, H. and J. G. C. Anderson (1922) *P. Cornelii Taciti de vita Agricolae*. Oxford.

Gordon, A. (1726) *Itinerarium Septentrionale*. London.

Grant, R. (1822) Memoir concerning the Roman progress in Scotland to the north of the Grampian Hills, *Archaeologia Scotica 2*, 31–42.

Grillone, A. (ed.) (1977) *Hygini de metatione castrorum*.

Guido, M. (1978) *Prehistoric and Roman Glass Beads in Britain and Ireland*. London.

Hanson, W. S. (1978) Roman campaigns north of the Forth-Clyde isthmus: the evidence of the temporary camps. *Proc. Soc. Antiq. Scotland 109*, 140–50.

——(1980a) The first Roman occupation of Scotland, in Hanson and Keppie 1980, 15–44.

——(1980b) Agricola on the Forth-Clyde isthmus, *Scottish Archaeol. Forum 12*, 55–68.

——(1987) *Agricola and the conquest of the North*. London.

Hanson, W. S., C. M. Daniels, J. N. Dore & J. P. Gillam (1979) The Agricolan supply base at Red House, Corbridge, *Archaeol. Aeliana 7* (5th series), 1–97.

Hanson, W. S. & L. J. F. Keppie (eds) (1980) *Roman Frontier Studies 1979: papers presented to the Twelfth International Congress of Roman Frontier Studies*. Oxford.

Hanson, W. S. & G. S. Maxwell (1980) An Agricolan *praesidium* on the Forth-Clyde isthmus (Mollins, Strathclyde), *Britannia 11*, 43–9.

——(1983) *Rome's North West Frontier; the Antonine Wall*. Edinburgh.

Harmand, J. (1967) *Une Campaigne Césarienne: Alesia*. Paris.

Henderson, A. A. R. (1984) From 83 to 1983: on the trail of Mons Graupius, in *The Deeside Field Club* 18, 23–9.

Henderson-Stewart, D. (1960) The Battle of Mons Graupius, *Trans. Ancient Monuments Soc. 8* (new series), 75–88.

Hind, J. G. F. (1974) Agricola's fleet and Portus Trucculensis, *Britannia 5*, 285–8.

Hind, J. G. F. (1983) Caledonia and its occupation under the Flavians, *Proc. Soc. Antiq. Scotland 113*, 373–8.

Horsley, J. (1732) *Britannia Romana*. London.

Jackson, K. H. (1956) The Pictish Language, in Wainwright 1956, 192–66.

Jarrett, M. G. (1982) Review of *Scottish Archaeol. Forum 12* in *The Antiquaries J. 62*, part 1, 420.

——(1985) History, Archaeology and Roman Scotland, *Proc. Soc. Antiq. Scotland 115*, 59–66.

Jones, G. D. B. (1986) A Roman military site at Cawdor, *Popular Archaeology 7*(3), 13–16.

Keegan, J. (1976) *The Face of Battle*. London.

Keillar, I. (1986) 'In fines Borestorum' – to the land of the Boresti, *Popular Archaeology 7*(3), 2–9.

Keppie, L. J. F. (1980) The search for a battlefield, in *Scottish Archaeol. Forum 12*, 79–88.

Keppie, L. J. F. (1979) *Roman Distance Slabs from the Antonine Wall: a brief guide*. Glasgow.

Longworth, I. H., D. R. Brothwell & R. Powers (1967) A massive cist with multiple burials of Iron Age date, *Proc. Soc. Antiq. Scotland 98*, 173–98.

Macdonald, G. (1916) Two Roman camps at Raedykes and Glenmailen, *Proc. Soc. Antiq. Scotland 50*, 317–59.

——(1919) The Agricolan occupation of north Britain, *J. Roman Studies 9*, 111–38.

——(1934) *The Roman Wall in Scotland*. Oxford.

——(1937) 'Britannia statim omissa', *J. Roman Studies 27*, 93–8.

MacGregor, M. (1976) *Early Celtic Art in Northern Britain*. Leicester.

Macinnes, L. (1982) Pattern and purpose: the settlement evidence, in *Later Prehistoric Settlement in South-east Scotland* (ed. D. W. Harding), 57–74. Edinburgh.

——(1984) Brochs and the Roman Occupation of lowland Scotland, *Proc. Soc. Antiq. Scotland 114*, 235–49.

MacKie, E. W. (1983) The Leckie broch, Stirlingshire: an interim report, *Glasgow Archaeol. J. 9*, 60–72.

Maitland, W. (1757) *History and Antiquities of Scotland*. London.

Marshall, D. N. (1977) Carved stone balls, *Proc. Soc. Antiq. Scotland 108* (1976–7), 40–72.

Maxwell, G. S. (1969) Excavations at Drumcarrow, Fife, *Proc. Soc. Antiq. Scotland 100*, 100–8.

——(1975) *Casus belli*: native pressures and Roman policy, *Scottish Archaeol. Forum 7*, 31–49.

——(1978) Air photography and the work of the Royal Commission, *Aerial Archaeol. 2*, 37–44.

——(1980) Agricola's campaigns: the evidence of the temporary camps, *Scottish Archaeol. Forum 12*, 25–54.

——(1982) Roman temporary camps at Inchtuthil: an examination of the aerial photographic evidence, *Scottish Archaeol. Rev. 1* (part 2), 105–13.

——(1983a) Cropmark categories observed in recent aerial reconnaissance in Scotland, *Scottish Archaeol. Rev. 2*, part 1, 45–52.

——(1983b) Recent aerial discoveries in Roman Scotland: Drumquhassle, Elginhaugh and Woodhead, *Britannia 14*, 167–82.

——(1983c) Recent aerial survey in Scotland, in *The Impact of Aerial Reconnaissance on Archaeology* (CBA Research Report No. 49; ed. G. S. Maxwell).

——(1983d) Roman settlement in Scotland, in *Settlement in North Britain 1000 BC-AD 1000* (B. A. R. British Series, 118; eds J. C. Chapman and H. C. Mytum), 233–61. Oxford.

——(1984a) Sidelight on the Roman military campaigns in north Britain, in *Studien zu den Militärgrenzen Roms III: 13 Internationaler Limeskongress, Aalen 1983, Vorträge* (ed. D. Planck), 60–3. Stuttgart.

——(1984b) 'New frontiers: the Roman Fort at Doune and its possible significance,' *Britannia 15*, 217–23.

——(1987) Settlement in southern Pictland: a new overview, in *The Picts: A New look at Old Problems* (ed. A. Small), 31–44. Dundee.

——(1989a) *The Romans in Scotland.* Edinburgh.

——(1989b) Flavian Frontiers in Caledonia, in *Proceedings of the Fourteenth International Congress of Roman Frontier Studies.* Vienna.

Maxwell, G. S. & D. R. Wilson (1987) Air Reconnaissance in Roman Britain, *Britannia 18*, 1–48.

Miller, Lt.-Col. (1857) An inquiry respecting the site of the battle of Mons Grampius, *Archaeol. Scotica 4*, 19–52.

Miller, N. P. (1969) Style and content in Tacitus, in Dorey 1969, 99–116.

Mitchell, A. (ed.) (1906) *Walter Macfarlane's geographical collections relating to Scotland.* Edinburgh.

Ogilvie, R. M. & I. A. Richmond (eds) (1967) *Cornelii Taciti de vita Agricolae.* Oxford.

Piggott, S. (1958) Native economies and the Roman occupation of North Britain, in *Roman and Native in North Britain* (ed. I. A. Richmond), 1–27. Edinburgh.

——(1983) *The Earliest Wheeled Transport.* London.

Pitblado, L. O. (1935) *The Roman Invasions: A Saga of the Caledonian Race.* London.

Pitts, L. F. & J. K. S. St Joseph (1985) *Inchtuthil: the Roman Legionary Fortress (Britannia* Monograph Series No. 6). London.

Playfair, J. (1797) The parish of Bendothy, Perthshire, in *The Statistical Account of Scotland 19*, 3–71. Edinburgh.

Powell, T. G. (1963) Some implications of chariotry, in *Culture and Environment* (eds I. Ll. Foster & L. Alcock), 153–69. London.

Potter, T. W. (1979) *The Romans in North-west England.* Kendal.

Prebble, J. (1967) *Culloden.* London.

RCAHMS (1978) *Lanarkshire: an Inventory of the Prehistoric and Roman Monuments.* Edinburgh.

RCAHMS (1982) *South Kincardine: Kincardine and Deeside District,*

Grampian Region. (The Archaeological Sites and Monuments of Scotland, 15). Edinburgh.

Rankin, H. D. (1987) *Celts and the Classical World.* London.

Reed, N. H. (1971) The fifth year of Agricola's campaigns, *Britannia 2*, 143–8.

Richmond, I. A. (1940) Excavations on the estate of Meikleour, Perthshire, 1939, *Proc. Soc. Antiq. Scotland 74*, 23–47.

Ritchie, J. N. G. (1969) Shields in north Britain in the Iron Age, *Scottish Archaeological Forum 1*, 31–40.

Rivet, A. L. F. & C. Smith (1979) *The Place-names of Roman Britain.* London.

Robertson, A. S. (1964) *The Roman Fort at Castledykes.* Edinburgh.

—— (1975) The Romans in north Britain: the coin evidence, in *Aufstieg and Niedergang der Römischen Welt II.3* (ed. H. Temporini) 364–428. Berlin.

Robinson, H. R. (1975) *The Armour of Imperial Rome.* London.

Roy, W. (1793) *The Military Antiquities of the Romans in North Britain.* London.

St Joseph, J. K. S. (1951) Air reconnaissance of north Britain, *J. Roman Stud. 41*, 52–65.

——(1961) Air reconnaissance in Britain 1958–60, *J. Roman Stud. 51*, 119–35.

——(1969) Air reconnaissance in Britain 1965–68, *J. Roman Stud. 59*, 104–28.

——(1973) Air reconnaissance in Roman Britain 1969–72, *J. Roman Stud. 63*, 214–46.

——(1976) Air reconnaissance of Roman Scotland, 1939–75, *Glasgow Archaeol. J. 4*, 1–28.

——(1978a) The camp at Durno and Mons Graupius, *Britannia 9*, 271–88.

——(1978b) Air reconnaissance: recent results, 44, *Antiquity 52*, 47–50.

St Joseph, J. K. S. & G. S. Maxwell (forthcoming) Excavation at the Roman fort at Cargill, *Britannia.*

Sibbald, R. (1707) *Historical Inquiries, concerning Roman Monuments and Antiquities in the North Part of Britain called Scotland.* Edinburgh.

——(1711) *Commentarius de Gestis Julii Agricolae in Scotia.* Edinburgh.

Small, A. (1823) *Interesting Roman Antiquities recently discovered in Fife.* Edinburgh.

Smith, I. G. (1987) *The First Roman Invasion of Scotland.* Edinburgh.

Smith, N. S. (1828) *A Dissertation on the Manners of the Germans with the Life of Agricola by Cornelius Tacitus translated from Brotier's Edition.* Oxford.

Stevenson, R. B. K. (1966) Metalwork and other objects in Scotland and their cultural affinities, in *The Iron Age in Northern Britain* (ed. A. L. F. Rivet), 17–44. Edinburgh.

Stuart, J. (1822) Observations upon the various accounts of the progress of the Roman arms in Scotland, and of the scene of the great battle between Agricola and Galgacus, *Archaeol. Scotica 2*, 289–313.

Stuart, J. (1868) Notice of letters addressed to Captain Shand, R. A., by Professor Thorkelin and General Robert Melvill, on Roman antiquities in the North of Scotland, 1788–90, *Proc. Soc. Antiq. Scotland 7*, 26–34.

Stuart, R. (1845) *Caledonia Romana: a Descriptive Account of the Roman Antiquities of Scotland*. (1st edn) Edinburgh.

Syme, R. (1932) Die Zahl der *Praefecti Castrorum* im Heere des Varus, *Germania 16*, 109–11.

Visy, Z. (1978) Der beginn der Donau-Kriege des Domitian, *Acta Archaeologica Academiae Scientiarum Hungaricae*, 30–2, 37–60.

Wainwright, F. T. (ed.) (1956) *The Problem of the Picts*. Edinburgh.

——(1963) *The Souterrains of Southern Pictland*. London.

Watson, W. J. (1926) *History of the Celtic Place-names of Scotland*. Edinburgh.

Webster, G. (1969) *The Roman Imperial Army of the First and Second Centuries A.D.* London.

Wellesley, K. (1969a) Review of Ogilvie and Richmond 1967, *J. Roman Stud.*, *59*, 266–9.

——(1969b) Tacitus as a military historian, in Dorey 1969, 63–97.

Whittington, G. (1975) Place names and the settlement pattern of Dark-age Scotland, *Proc. Soc. Antiq. Scotland 106*, 99–110.

Wilson, D. R. (1983) *Air Photo Interpretation for Archaeologists*. London.

Index

Only main references to Agricola and Tacitus are indexed.
Italicised entries for *Agricola* refer to The *Agricola* of Tacitus.